DURHAM PUBLIC LIBRARY

W9-AFX-246

DISCARD

Women of Achievement

Michelle Obama

Women of Achievement

Abigail Adams
Susan B. Anthony
Tyra Banks
Clara Barton
Hillary Rodham Clinton
Marie Curie
Ellen DeGeneres
Diana, Princess of Wales
Tina Fey
Ruth Bader Ginsburg
Joan of Arc
Helen Keller
Madonna
Michelle Obama
Sandra Day O'Connor
Georgia O'Keeffe
Nancy Pelosi
Rachael Ray
Anita Roddick
Eleanor Roosevelt
Martha Stewart
Barbara Walters
Venus and Serena Williams

Women of Achievement

Michelle Obama

FIRST LADY

Paul McCaffrey

CHELSEA HOUSE
PUBLISHERS
An imprint of Infobase Publishing

MICHELLE OBAMA

Copyright © 2011 by Infobase Publishing

All rights reserved. No part of this book may be reproduced or utilized in any form or by any means, electronic or mechanical, including photocopying, recording, or by any information storage or retrieval systems, without permission in writing from the publisher. For information, contact:

Chelsea House
An imprint of Infobase Publishing
132 West 31st Street
New York NY 10001

Library of Congress Cataloging-in-Publication Data
McCaffrey, Paul, 1977-
  Michelle Obama : First Lady / Paul McCaffrey.
  p. cm. — (Women of achievement)
  Includes bibliographical references and index.
  ISBN 978-1-60413-911-2 (hardcover)
  1. Obama, Michelle, 1964—Juvenile literature. 2. Presidents' spouses—United States—Biography—Juvenile literature. 3. Legislators' spouses—United States—Biography—Juvenile literature. 4. African American women lawyers—Illinois—Chicago—Biography—Juvenile literature. 5. Chicago (Ill.)—Biography—Juvenile literature. I. Title. II. Series.

  E909.O24M39 2010
  973.932092—dc22
  [B]
                          2010019915

Chelsea House books are available at special discounts when purchased in bulk quantities for businesses, associations, institutions, or sales promotions. Please call our Special Sales Department in New York at (212) 967-8800 or (800) 322-8755.

You can find Chelsea House on the World Wide Web at http://www.chelseahouse.com.

Text design Erik Lindstrom
Cover design by Ben Peterson and Alicia Post
Composition by A Good Thing
Cover printed by Bang Printing, Brainerd, MN
Book printed and bound by Bang Printing, Brainerd, MN
Date printed: December 2010

10 9 8 7 6 5 4 3 2 1

This book is printed on acid-free paper.

All links and Web addresses were checked and verified to be correct at the time of publication. Because of the dynamic nature of the Web, some addresses and links may have changed since publication and may no longer be valid.

CONTENTS

An Election
for the Ages

On November 4, 2008, Michelle and Barack Obama arrived at Beulah Shoesmith Elementary School on the South Side of Chicago, Illinois, at about 7:30 A.M. They had spent the past year and a half crisscrossing the country campaigning for the presidency. What had once seemed like a long shot—a freshman African-American senator seeking to become president of the United States—had culminated in Barack's nomination on the Democratic Party's ticket. Now, on Election Day 2008, they had returned to the Windy City to cast their ballots. It was a fitting location for this moment in their journey together. The school was not far from the tidy brick bungalow where Michelle had grown up, the housing projects where Barack first worked as a community organizer, and the law firm where the aspiring first

On November 4, 2008, the Democratic presidential nominee, Senator Barack Obama of Illinois, and his wife, Michelle Obama, carry their ballots to the voting booth in their hometown of Chicago, Illinois. Senator Obama would go on to beat the Republican nominee, Senator John McCain of Arizona, later that day.

couple had met. Michelle entered the voting booth. Basking in the moment, she stood there for a time, reflecting on the extraordinary events and the many sacrifices that had brought them to this point. She thought about her father, Fraser Robinson III, who first went to work full time at the age of 11 to support his family and who, though stricken with a debilitating disease, rose early every morning so that his children might have a better life. She thought about her two daughters, Sasha and Malia, and what this day meant for them. And she thought about the nation and the difficult challenges that lay ahead. After casting her vote, she walked out and rejoined her husband.

That night, after a steak dinner, the Obamas headed to a suite at the Chicago Hyatt Regency hotel. Together with family, friends, and campaign staff, they huddled around the television to watch the election returns. When the news networks declared that Barack had won the state of Ohio, the candidate looked to his top adviser, David Axelrod, and asked, "So it looks like we're gonna win this thing, huh?" Axelrod replied, "It looks like it, yeah."[1]

At about 11 P.M., the news became official: Barack Obama would be the next president of the United States. Despite their victory, those gathered in the suite were restrained. Instead of celebrating, they were grave and serious, mindful of the tremendous responsibility that would now be Barack's to shoulder. For her part, Michelle stated, "I was proud as a wife, amazed as a citizen. I felt a sense of relief, a sense of calm that the country I lived in was the country I thought I lived in."[2]

Every four years, Americans head to the polls to elect a president, and although every election is unique, the 2008 contest was truly one for the history books. For the first time in the 200-plus years of the United States, an African American was on the ballot representing one of the two major American political parties. And he had won. Setting aside the politics and the issues of the 2008 election, for a nation that had endured slavery, the Civil War, Reconstruction, and Jim Crow, that Barack and Michelle Obama would now hold the keys to the White House stood as a powerful testament to American progress and the ability of a nation and a people to overcome.

GRANT PARK

Later that night, the Obamas headed to Chicago's Grant Park where more than 200,000 supporters were waiting. In the crowd, many were weeping with joy. A cheer went up as Barack, Michelle, Sasha, and Malia Obama walked onstage. Addressing the nation and those watching around the world, the president-elect began, "If there is anyone out there who still doubts that America is a place where all things are possible; who still wonders if the dream of our founders is alive in our time; who still questions the power of our democracy, tonight is your answer."[3]

Already recognized for his skill as a speaker, Barack exceeded his own high standards in his victory address. He saved some of his most eloquent words for his wife. "I would not be standing here tonight," he intoned, "without the unyielding support of my best friend for the last sixteen years—the rock of our family and the love of my life, our nation's next first lady, Michelle Obama."[4]

Dressed in a black-and-red silk and satin dress, Michelle stood with her daughters and waved to the adoring crowd. Michelle had proven herself on the campaign trail. She had endured the criticism and the personal attacks, the rumor and innuendo. She had made mistakes, but she had learned from them. With her wit and down-to-earth charm, she had served as one of her husband's most effective boosters. Not only did she win over voters, helping convince them to cast their ballots for Barack, she emerged during the campaign

President-elect Barack Obama acknowledges his supporters along with his wife, Michelle, and daughters, Malia (*second from right*) and Sasha, during an election night gathering in Grant Park in Chicago, on November 4, 2008.

as one of the nation's most accomplished and fascinating people.

Her path to Grant Park that November night had been long and difficult. Unlike many first ladies, Michelle did not enjoy a wealthy or privileged upbringing. Her origins were humble. Her ancestors had not arrived in the United States seeking a better life or fleeing religious persecution. They had been brought to America to work the fields as slaves. Over the generations they persevered, from the plantations of the South, eventually making their way to the gritty streets of Chicago's South Side.

From these modest beginnings, like her forebears before her, Michelle made the most of the opportunities available to her. She sought out the most challenging schools, intent on realizing her full potential. Spurred on by the inspiring example set by her parents, she tackled her studies with single-minded intensity.

Her efforts paid off. From Whitney Young High School in Chicago, Michelle followed her brother, Craig, into the Ivy League when she was accepted at Princeton University. From Princeton she went on to Harvard Law School and then began a career as a corporate attorney at the Chicago firm of Sidley & Austin, where she met her future husband. Unsatisfied with corporate law, Michelle left her high-paying position to serve the public, first working in economic development for the city of Chicago and then for the nonprofit organization (NPO) Public Allies, where she prepared students for careers in public service. After building the Chicago branch of Public Allies, Michelle worked in community relations for the University of Chicago and later for the University of Chicago Hospitals, helping to break down long-standing divisions between these organizations and the surrounding community.

"I believe," she observed, "that each of us—no matter what our age or background or walk of life—each of us has something to contribute to the life of this nation." As an attorney, wife, mother, and now as first lady, Michelle Obama has sought to live those words. Her story stands as a powerful testament to the idea that "the only limit to the height of your achievements is the reach of your dreams and your willingness to work for them."[5]

The Shieldses, the Robinsons, and the Great Migration

Michelle Obama was born Michelle LaVaughn Robinson on January 17, 1964, in Chicago, Illinois, the second child of Fraser Robinson III and the former Marian Lois Shields. Michelle's older brother, Craig, had been born 21 months earlier. Michelle's parents gave her the middle name LaVaughn after Fraser III's mother. Though much of their history had been lost, remembering where they came from was important to the Robinson family. The family's journey had been a difficult one, the modest security they had achieved on the South Side of Chicago hard earned, built on the faith and sacrifice of earlier generations.

THE ROBINSONS

Fraser Robinson III's family hailed from South Carolina. His father, Fraser Jr., was born on the coast, in a town called Georgetown, in what is now Georgetown County. Georgetown itself is located about 60 miles (96.5 kilometers) northeast of Charleston, on Winyah Bay, where three rivers—the Sampit, the Pee Dee, and the Waccamaw—meet and empty into the Atlantic Ocean. Fraser Jr. moved to Chicago sometime before his son's birth in 1935, as part of one of the largest mass movements of people in history: the Great Migration, in which millions of African Americans moved from the South to the industrial cities of the North. He had difficulty finding a job and was forced to leave his wife and children for long periods. During these absences, the family had to turn to public assistance.

After Fraser Jr. served in the army during World War II, he was hired as a postal clerk in Chicago. Just before Michelle's parents were married, Fraser III was living in a cinder-block housing project with his wife, the former LaVaughn Delores Johnson, who worked in a religious bookstore. After his retirement, Fraser Jr. moved with LaVaughn back to Georgetown, where he rejoined the Bethel AME Church at which he had worshipped as a child. Recalling her grandfather, Michelle remarked, "He was a very proud man. He was proud of his lineage [but] there was a discontent about him."[1]

THE "LOW COUNTRY"

The Robinsons had deep roots not only in Georgetown but also in the surrounding region. Georgetown sat in what is known as the "Low Country" of South Carolina, a marshy area that once produced some of the largest fortunes in colonial America. Much of the Low Country was below sea level, where flooding was common. This geography, along with the humid climate, made the area perfect for rice farming. At one point the region grew nearly half of all the rice in the

A giant oak tree near an antebellum house at the Hofwyl-Broadfield Plantation State Historic Site in Georgia. Michelle Obama's ancestors worked on such plantations in Georgia and South Carolina as slaves before the Civil War.

United States and created vast wealth for the owners of the rice plantations.

Growing rice, however, required a lot of work, more than many other crops. Intricate systems of canals and drainage ditches needed to be constructed and tended for the crop to prosper. Harvesting the rice took enormous effort as well. The heavy crop was difficult to transport across the muddy landscape. There were other drawbacks. What made the region great for growing rice also created ideal conditions for alligators and venomous snakes, as well as diseases like malaria and yellow fever. On a daily basis, those working the rice fields faced a number of potential threats that could take their lives.

The inhabitants of Georgetown County—or All Saints Parish as it was called in colonial times—were overwhelmingly black. During the course of the year, the population varied between 85 and 98 percent African American, peaking in the hot summer months—prime malaria season—when most of the white people in the area left for more pleasant climes. These early African Americans, including the first lady's forebears, were slaves. Since the population of the Low Country was so uniformly black, with many coming from the same region of Africa, a local culture and language called Gullah developed there, which preserved many African traditions and remains an important part of African American culture in the United States up until this day.

Those African slaves imported to Georgetown and the Low Country came mostly from an area that slave traders referred to as the "rice coast."[2] Located in modern-day Sierra Leone, Gambia, and Senegal, this region earned its name because rice farming was common there. Because its climate and terrain were similar to the Low Country, its inhabitants were believed to have built up immunity to such illnesses as malaria over the generations, which made them even more attractive to the rice growers in South Carolina.

JIM ROBINSON

Michelle Obama's great-great-grandfather, Jim Robinson, was born into slavery in about 1850. He may have been born at Friendfield, a 500-acre (202.3-hectare) rice plantation near Georgetown, or his owner may have brought him there. The property of the Withers family, Friendfield had been in operation for 100 years before Jim Robinson came to work its fields. The main house and surrounding gardens were famous for their grandeur. The Withers' property included six plantations and more than 500 slaves. The slave population at Friendfield, on the eve of the Civil War, numbered 273.

The slaves at Friendfield lived in three strips of cabins along Slave Street. The rows of slaves' quarters ran parallel to one another and each row consisted of about 10 buildings. The individual houses were home to several families and included a fireplace and an attic. In 1841, the plantation owner, Francis Withers, built a church for the slaves. Upon his death in 1847, Francis Withers left his family $10,000 to buy more slaves for the plantation and asked that they treat all the slaves kindly.

Before the Civil War, Friendfield was among the most successful and wealthy plantations in the area. After that brutal conflict ruined the economy of the South, Friendfield fell on hard times. The plantation's rice mill was destroyed by fire, the main house ravaged by looters. Then a smallpox epidemic broke out. By 1879, the Withers family started selling off property.

Though freed from slavery, Jim Robinson stayed on at the plantation as a farmer after the Civil War. His wife gave birth to two sons, first Gabriel, then, in 1884, Fraser Sr., Michelle's great-grandfather. Fraser's mother died when he was young, and Jim Robinson soon remarried.

FRASER SR.

At 10 years old, according to family lore, Fraser Sr. went into the forest to gather firewood. While in the woods, a tree fell on his arm and broke it. His stepmother did not think the injury serious. The wound became infected, and before long the arm had to be amputated.

A white man from Georgetown, Francis Nesmith, grew fond of the one-armed boy and asked Jim Robinson if Fraser might come live with him and his family, promising to take good care of him. Jim Robinson agreed, and Fraser moved in with the Nesmiths. While residing with the Nesmiths, Fraser learned to read and write.

In this newspaper illustration by James E. Taylor, *Shipping Rice from a Plantation on the Savannah River,* black laborers are seen carting rice to boats. Known as the "rice coast," Georgetown and the Low Country were home to African slaves brought to South Carolina to work the rice fields.

Though the son of a slave, Fraser Robinson Sr. was successful for his time and place; he worked at a lumber mill and as a shoemaker and newspaper salesman. He married Rosella Cohen, sometimes spelled Rose Ella, by whom he had at least six children. In 1912, Rosella gave birth to Michelle's grandfather, Fraser Jr.

During World War I, Fraser Sr. registered for the draft but was unable to serve due to his missing arm. As a newspaper salesman in Georgetown, Fraser Sr. always brought home copies of the paper to teach his children how to read. Fraser Jr. eventually graduated from high school. According to the 1930 census, Fraser Jr. lived at home and worked in a lumber mill, the Atlantic Coast Lumber Company, Georgetown's largest employer. He also developed a reputation as a gifted speaker.

At about this time, conditions for the African Americans in the area were deteriorating. The Great Depression—a severe worldwide economic downturn that lasted throughout the 1930s—had destroyed the local economy, taking down the lumber mill, while Jim Crow laws were constricting the freedoms of the area's black citizens. Hoping for a better future, Fraser Jr. soon made the decision to head north, joining what would come to be called the Great Migration. He followed a family friend to Chicago, where he would meet and marry Michelle's grandmother and raise his family, including Michelle's father, Fraser III.

THE SHIELDSES

The story of Michelle Obama's maternal ancestors, the Shieldses, has much in common with that of the Robinsons. Like the Robinsons, her mother Marian's family overcame

(continues on page 22)

IN HER OWN WORDS

In a 2008 interview with Shailagh Murray, Michelle Obama discussed her heritage extensively, saying in part:

> It makes more sense to me . . . if the patriarch in our lineage was one-armed Fraser, a shoemaker with one arm, an entrepreneur, someone who was able to own property, and with sheer effort and determination was able to build a life in this town—that must have been the messages that my grandfather got.*

* Shailagh Murray, "A Family Tree Rooted in American Soil," *Washington Post*, October 2, 2008, http://www.washingtonpost.com/wp-dyn/content/story/2008/10/01/ST2008100103245.html.

THE GREAT MIGRATION

In 1910, the United States was home to 8 million African Americans. Of these, 7 million resided in the South. Over the next 15 years, 1 in 10 of these 7 million would move north, a trend that continued at different speeds over the next several generations. This mass exodus became known as the Great Migration. While historians do not always agree on the migration's exact dates and numbers (with some holding that there were two distinct "great" migrations), the basic facts are that between roughly 1910 and 1970, a total of approximately 7 million African Americans made the journey north.

The reasons for this migration were numerous. In the years just after the Civil War (1861–1865), African Americans were freed from slavery and enjoyed all the benefits of full citizenship. During Reconstruction (1865–1877), their newly won rights were protected by federal troops occupying the defeated Southern states. Following the disputed presidential election of 1876, however, Reconstruction came to an end and African Americans in the South saw these rights and safeguards diminished. Between 1890 and 1910, in particular, Jim Crow laws were passed throughout the former Confederate and Border states that restricted the right of African Americans to vote. This legal framework for the system of segregation would last into the 1960s. Discrimination also took more frightening forms, as racial violence was commonplace. The Klu Klux Klan (KKK) and lynching were facts of life throughout the nation but especially in the South. Such dangers convinced many black Americans to head north in hopes of finding a safer place to call home. Unfortunately, their new neighbors often proved as unwelcoming as the ones who were left behind.

More than discrimination, the quest for economic opportunity drove the Great Migration. Northern states had always been far more industrialized than those in the South. Farming, that of cotton especially, and slave labor were the foundations of the Southern economy. What little industrial development had taken place there was soon destroyed in the Civil War. After the war, the South returned to its agricultural roots. As factories opened up throughout the North, farming—and cotton—remained king in the South. This served to keep the region poorer and less educated.

In 1898, the boll weevil beetle appeared in Texas and gradually spread throughout the South. In 1915 and 1916, it destroyed much of the cotton harvest. The poverty this created persuaded many African Americans, who had been employed in cotton farming since the days of slavery, to head north, where workers were needed to man the factories. At about the time of World War I, the steady, six-decades-long flow of immigrants from Europe into the United States had dried up, resulting in a labor shortage just as U.S. factories needed to ramp up production.

The labor shortage grew worse in 1917, when the United States entered the war. With men leaving the assembly line for the armed forces and the U.S. government looking to supply them, the factories needed new workers. African Americans from the South stepped up, moving from the barren cotton fields to the assembly line.

This massive migration transformed the industrial cities of the North. In New York, Chicago, Philadelphia, and Detroit, the African-American population skyrocketed by 66, 148, 500, and 611 percent, respectively, between 1910 and 1920. The changes did not come easily. Racial violence regularly flared up as African-American newcomers were blamed for low wages and a host of other ills. In many cities, the effects of the Great Migration, the struggle to integrate rather than segregate, continued.

(continued from page 19)

slavery and discrimination to obtain a small piece of the American Dream. The first Shields of whom there is a substantial public record is Melvinia. Melvinia first appears in the 1850 will of David Patterson, a South Carolina slave owner, who, in dividing his possessions, refers to the then six-year-old slave, one of 21 that he owned, as the "negro girl Melvinia."[3] She was valued at $475. Following her owner's death in 1852, Melvinia was uprooted and sent to Georgia, where she went to live with Christianne and Henry Shields, her former owner's daughter and son-in-law, on their 200-acre (80.9 ha) farm in the town of Rex, outside Atlanta.

In 1859, Melvinia bore a son, Dolphus T. Shields, while she was in her midteens. The child's father was a white man. No record exists of just who this man was. It could have been Henry Shields himself. Or it could have been one of his four sons, who were between the ages of 19 and 24 at the time, or someone else. Whoever this man was, he and Melvinia are the first lady's great-great-great-grandparents. We can only speculate as to their connection and whether their relationship was entered into freely.

By 1870, Melvinia was free and working as a farmer on land next to Charles Shields, a son of Henry Shields, her former owner. Melvinia had four children, three of whom were listed as "mulatto," what we today call biracial, on the census of that year. Melvinia gave all of her children the last name Shields. This may indicate that a Shields fathered some of them, or simply that Melvinia followed the tradition of the time, naming her children after her master or former master. One of these biracial children was born several years after the slaves were freed during the Civil War, suggesting that the relationship that produced Melvinia's mixed-race offspring endured beyond the end of slavery.

Sometime in the 1870s or 1880s, Melvinia moved west to Bartow County, on the border with Alabama, where she reunited with Mariah and Bolus Easley, both former Patterson slaves from her childhood in South Carolina. Melvinia lived into her nineties, passing away in 1938. According to her death certificate, which a relative signed, the names of her mother and father were listed as unknown: Melvinia may never have known who her parents were, the system of slavery shattering even the most basic of human relationships.

DOLPHUS SHIELDS

Dolphus Shields married Michelle's great-great-grand-mother Alice Easley, a daughter of Mariah and Bolus. Sometime before 1888, he moved with her to Birmingham, Alabama, where he worked as a carpenter and tool sharpener. According to the census of 1900, he owned his own house in a black, working-class section of the city. By 1911, he had started his own business, which was located in the white part of town.

Dolphus was a deeply religious man and was one of the founders of First Ebenezer Baptist Church and Trinity Baptist Church in Birmingham. He served as a Sunday school teacher and forbade swearing, smoking, and other vices in his home. Women were not allowed to wear makeup or pants. The only music that could be listened to was religious hymns.

Dolphus and Alice eventually separated. She earned her living as a maid and seamstress. Recalling Dolphus Shields, Helen Heath, who knew him from church, commented, "He was the dean of the deacons in Birmingham. He was a serious man. He was about business." He did not talk about his ancestry, however. "We got to the place where we didn't want anybody to know we knew slaves; people didn't want to talk about that."[4]

ROBERT LEE AND PURNELL SHIELDS

One of Dolphus and Alice's children was Robert Lee Shields, Michelle's great-grandfather, who was born around 1885. In 1906, he married Anna ("Annie") Estelle Lawson or "Laws", who in 1910 bore him a son, Purnell Nathaniel Shields, the first lady's maternal grandfather. Robert Lee worked as a painter, a railroad porter, and a laborer, but by his thirty-second birthday, he disappears from the public record. Sometime in the early 1920s, Annie Lawson moved her family to Chicago, where she worked as a seamstress and married a tailor named Frank Coleman.

Purnell Shields worked as a painter and, according to the 1930 census, at a syrup factory. He married Michelle's grandmother, Rebecca Jumper (or Coleman), who was born in 1909 and served as a nurse at Chicago's Grant Hospital. Rebecca and Purnell would have eight children in total. Marian, the first lady's mother, was born in 1937.

From slavery in South Carolina, the Robinsons and the Shieldses, Michelle Obama's ancestors, followed different paths on the journey that would ultimately bring them together. For generations, the Robinsons stayed close to their South Carolina roots in Georgetown, until Fraser Jr. decided to try his luck in Chicago. The Shieldses, on the other hand, were blown all across the South, from South Carolina to Georgia to Alabama, before Annie Lawson took her family to Chicago. It was in the Windy City, on Chicago's legendary South Side, that the Shieldses and the Robinsons would finally come together. Reflecting on her family's American odyssey, Michelle commented:

> An important message in this journey is that we're all linked. Somewhere there was a slave owner—or a white family in my great-grandfather's time that gave him a place, a home, that helped him build a life—that again led to me. So who were those

people? I would argue they're just as much a part of my history as my great-grandfather. . . . There are probably thousands of one-armed Frasers, all over this country, who, out of slavery and emancipation, because they were smart and worked hard, those American values, were able to lift themselves up.[5]

In her own life, Michelle Obama, through a combination of determination and talent, would continue this family tradition, lifting herself up and setting an example that her ancestors would find familiar.

South Side Roots

Like many who had made the journey north during the Great Migration, the Shieldses and the Robinsons had not found the prosperity they had longed for. Raised on the South Side, Fraser III went to work on a milk truck at the age of 11 in order to support his family. Despite the burden of these responsibilities, he graduated from high school and even began his college education before money troubles forced him to drop out. And as one of eight children in a working-class family, Marian Shields also knew what it meant to go without. She and Fraser III were from the same South Side neighborhood. They first met in high school and married in 1960. Together they worked to build their children a home that was free from the want they had known.

Three days before Michelle's birth on January 17, 1964, her father, Fraser III, was hired as a "station laborer"[1] by the water department of the city of Chicago at a salary of $479 a month. The job could not have come at a better time. Before Michelle's brother, Craig, had been born, Marian worked as a secretary at the Sears Roebuck Catalog Company but left to take care of her growing family. When she became pregnant with Michelle, she feared that she would need to get a job to help support the family. Thankfully, Fraser III's position at the water department meant that Marian could stay home and raise the children. Though in his new job he would at first perform the duties of a janitor, mopping floors and picking up trash, Fraser had cause to be thankful. For an African-American man in 1964 Chicago—indeed, 1964 America—there were few better prospects. Discrimination was all too common and one could not realistically aim much higher. As a government employee, however, Fraser would receive a steady income, pension benefits, vacation time, and guaranteed tenure, meaning that he could not be easily fired or laid off. This gave the Robinsons the sort of security of which most African-American families of their day could only dream.

PRECINCT POLITICS

In addition to his job with the water department, Fraser also served as a volunteer precinct captain for the Democratic Party. That he was involved in the Democratic Party and worked for the city was probably not a coincidence. Long a stronghold of the Democratic Party, Chicago, under Mayor Richard J. Daley, was home to one of the most notorious political machines in twentieth-century America. Daley was first elected in 1955 and served until his death in 1976. Daley's Chicago machine was built on patronage. If you wanted the best city services and access to city jobs, you needed to deliver the votes, making sure the people in your precinct showed up at the polls and cast their ballots for the right candidates. This sort of system was not unique to Chicago, yet Chicago was where it was practiced most effectively.

The precinct captains played an important role in the machine. In general, they were respected and popular members of their communities. They made the rounds of the local funerals, weddings, and celebrations, shaking hands and keeping their fingers on the pulse of their neigh-

THE SOUTH SIDE OF CHICAGO

During the Great Migration, approximately 500,000 African Americans settled in Chicago, most of them on the South Side, an area located south of the Chicago River and outside the city's downtown Loop. Lured by the promise of work in Chicago's stockyards, steel mills, and packinghouses, these newcomers transformed the city and made the South Side into one of the richest and most vibrant African-American communities in the United States. From the South Side would come the distinct sound of Chicago Blues and the cultural achievements of the Chicago Black Renaissance, including the works of writers like Richard Wright, Gwendolyn Brooks, and Margaret Walker.

That huge numbers of black Americans settled on the South Side was not by chance. Faced with this wave of newcomers and mindful of the ethnic strife that it could cause, Chicago's leaders channeled these migrants into the South Side and, to a lesser extent, the West Side. Government regulations, business practices, and the habits of the area's neighboring ethnic communities served to keep African Americans confined to a few selected communities. Realtors generally refused to show blacks homes in white areas. Few banks would give a black family the

borhoods. They would also pass out campaign literature and encourage people to vote for the machine's candidates. They also worked as middlemen between their communities and city services. If a traffic light needed to be fixed or a street snowplowed, the precinct captain was the person to see. Politics in Chicago was strictly a local affair.

With his sense of humor and friendly nature, Fraser III had the qualities of a great precinct captain. Michelle recalled:

mortgage loan to buy in a white area, and many neighborhoods had covenants stating that homes could not be sold to minorities. In many ways, the system of segregation in Chicago was similar to that found in the South; however, Chicago's immigrant communities—Irish, Italian, and Eastern European—added another layer of division on top of the black–white divide.

While many came to view the South Side as largely poor and black, the community was quite diverse, with poor as well as affluent and middle-class areas. Moreover, not only was the renowned University of Chicago located on the South Side, but so too was Bridgeport, a vast Irish-American neighborhood that served as the home base of Mayor Richard J. Daley.

Still, isolated from the rest of the city, the black residents of the South Side did not receive their share of city services. Given that they could only live in a few crowded communities, landlords could charge them more in rent and not bother to make repairs. Despite these shortcomings, African Americans in the South Side managed to achieve a level of prosperity they could not have hoped for in the South, and their cultural contributions shaped the larger black experience in the United States.

Some of my earliest memories are of tagging along with him as we'd walk door to door and help folks register to vote. We'd sit in neighbors' kitchens for hours and listen to their opinions, their concerns, and the dreams they had for their children. And before we left those kitchens, my father would make sure that everyone could get to the voting booth on Election Day—because he knew that a single vote could help make their dreams a reality.[2]

Although serving in the machine no doubt helped Fraser III in his career, it also forced him to compromise his ideals. The machine was imperfect and corrupt. As an African American, Fraser III knew this all too well. He knew the machine served to keep the city segregated. He knew that black Chicagoans could only climb so high in it. That they could not hope to move out of the city's South and West Sides, that their schools were crumbling and poorly funded, and the municipal services they received were second rate. Consequently, Fraser III may have been part of the machine, but he was not defined by it. According to Michelle's brother, "We as a family were extremely cynical about politics and politicians."[3]

Despite the Daley machine's flaws, for a city like Chicago, which had deep racial and ethnic tensions, it managed to keep an uneasy peace. The city itself is divided into 50 wards, or neighborhoods. In Fraser III's day, these neighborhoods were intensely segregated. The Polish stayed in their communities, the Irish, Italian, and blacks in theirs. Mistrust of outsiders was common. It could be dangerous to venture outside one's local community. Indeed, in 1966, Martin Luther King Jr. led a peaceful march to protest housing segregation in the city. The march entered a white neighborhood on Chicago's Southwest Side where it was met by an angry mob. The marchers were pelted

Mayor Richard J. Daley walks through Chicago in this circa-1960 photograph. Daley was mayor of Chicago for more than 20 years and ran one of the most powerful political machines in the United States.

with stones, firecrackers, and bottles. King described the racial hatred he encountered as the worst he had ever seen. Uniting such a divided city was next to impossible, but the machine made sure everyone depended on it.

MULTIPLE SCLEROSIS

When Michelle was still a toddler, her father came down with multiple sclerosis (MS), a disease that attacks the brain and spinal cord. MS interferes with the transmission of signals from the brain and spinal column to the rest of the body. Those suffering from it can display a number of different symptoms, from fatigue and vision problems to depression and difficulty walking. In some cases, it can be permanently disabling. Some forms of MS are progressive, meaning they grow worse over time. Fraser III's was such a case. Despite this, he dealt with it with inspiring perseverance, setting an example for his children that would stick with them throughout their lives. Michelle remembered:

> As he got sicker, it got harder for him to walk. It took him longer to get dressed in the morning. But if he was in pain, he never let on. He never stopped smiling and laughing, even while struggling to button his shirt, even while using two canes to get himself across the room to give my mom a kiss. He just woke up a little earlier and he worked a little harder.[4]

Fraser III did not let MS interfere with his career at the water department or his duties as a precinct captain. Though his condition gave him plenty of reason to slow down, he refused to give anything but 100 percent. "He got up and went to work every day. That's what I saw," Michelle recollected. He was "a man who didn't complain, was never late, never expressed any level of doubt about his situation in his life, and taught us that we could dream of anything."[5]

Fraser's illness and how he dealt with it taught his children the value of hard work and determination. Yet that was not all they learned. Much as he adapted to his condition, Fraser III could not completely shield his family from its toll. Growing up, Craig and Michelle had to adjust their lives to help care for their father. "When you have a parent with a disability," Michelle stated, "control and structure become critical habits, just to get through the day."[6] As a teenager, Craig would conduct fire drills, planning how he would transport his father from the burning house. From an early age, Craig and Michelle had to take responsibility for themselves and their family.

Seeing all the sacrifices their father made, Craig and Michelle were afraid of disappointing him. Although it was often left to Marian to discipline the two children if they misbehaved, Fraser III could bring them both to tears with a mere look. "We always felt we couldn't let Dad down because he worked so hard for us," Craig explained. "My sister and I, if one of us ever got in trouble with my father, we'd both be crying. We'd both be like, 'Oh, my God, Dad's upset. How could we do this to him?'"[7]

SOUTH SHORE

Despite his battle with MS, Fraser III's career with the water department went well. In 1968, he was promoted to foreman, with an increase in pay of almost $200 per month. That same year, he was named a "stationary fireman," overseeing one of the city's boilers. The following year he received another promotion, to "operating engineer." As he advanced, Fraser was able to move his young family from an apartment on the South Side to a house in the South Side neighborhood of South Shore.

Their house was located at 7436 South Euclid Avenue. Constructed of brick, the two-story bungalow was owned by Fraser III's aunt, a piano teacher, who lived on the first floor. Michelle and her family squeezed into the second floor. For a family of four, the living quarters were a bit on the small side. So that Craig and Michelle could have their own rooms, they constructed walls in the living room, giving each of them a cozy space to themselves. A friend of Michelle's described her room as "like a closet. . . . the smallest room I had ever seen."[8] This didn't stop Michelle from squeezing an Easy-Bake Oven and a dollhouse into it. Michelle also enjoyed playing with African-American Barbie dolls.

Because the house sat near a park and South Euclid Avenue did not have much traffic, Michelle and her brother could ride their bikes and roam the neighborhood

IN HER OWN WORDS

At a campaign rally in New Hampshire during the 2008 presidential election, Michelle Obama recalled:

Deep down inside, I'm still that little girl who grew up on the South Side of Chicago. I am a product of that experience through and through. Everything that I think about and do is shaped around the life that I lived in that little apartment in that bungalow my father worked so hard to provide for us.*

* Associated Press, April 4, 2008, http://www.news24.com/World/USElections/Michelle-Obama-the-superstar-20080330.

freely. At home, the Robinsons played Chinese checkers, chess, Monopoly, and other board games. Michelle was a tough competitor. Recalling their fierce battles over the Monopoly board, Craig commented that they had to "let her win enough that she wouldn't quit." Indeed, he added, "My sister is a poor sport. She doesn't like to lose."[9] Michelle's competitive streak was noticed by her mother as well. "She wanted to do the right thing all the time without being told, and she wanted to be the best at things," Marian remarked. "She liked winning."[10]

Marian and Fraser III only allowed their children one hour of television per day. Michelle, nicknamed "Miche"[11] by her brother, made the most of that time, committing all the episodes of *The Brady Bunch* to memory, while also enjoying *The Mary Tyler Moore Show* and *The Dick Van Dyke Show*. Michelle took piano lessons from her aunt and never needed any encouragement to practice. She would play for hours on end until her mother finally had to ask her to stop.

Fraser III and Marian also made sure Michelle and her brother contributed to keeping up the household. "We alternated washing dishes," Craig recalled. "I had Monday, Wednesday, Friday. Michelle had Tuesday, Thursday, Saturday."[12] The family shared one bathroom, and every Saturday it was Michelle's job to clean it.

After Fraser III's parents moved back to Georgetown in 1974, the family would drive to South Carolina during the summers to visit. A city girl, Michelle had trouble adjusting to the sounds of crickets late at night as she was falling asleep. They also vacationed in White Cloud, Michigan, at Duke's Happy Holiday Resort. A three- or four- hour drive from Chicago, Duke's was a popular destination spot for the city's black residents. The Robinsons would stay in White Cloud for up to a week.

EDUCATION

Though circumstances had prevented both Marian and Fraser III from completing college, it was not due to a lack of talent. They both had skipped the second grade and appreciated the value of education, encouraging their children to excel in the classroom. By the time Craig and Michelle were four years old, their mother had already taught them how to read. Michelle did not take to her mother's instruction very well at first. "She thought she could figure out how to read on her own, but she was too young to say that, so she just ignored me,"[13] Marian remembered. The Robinsons wanted their children to succeed and they often asked a lot of them. Describing her parenting philosophy, Marian stated, "If you aren't challenged, you don't make any progress."[14]

Before her children started kindergarten, Marian gave both of them their own alarm clocks, telling them: "You are becoming responsible for your own life. You have to see that you get up and give yourself enough time to eat breakfast and get yourself ready."[15] Craig took to this arrangement easily, leaping out of bed as soon as the alarm went off. Michelle, however, would ask her brother to wake her up when he was done using the bathroom.

Two years older than Michelle, Craig excelled in school. When it was Michelle's turn to start at Bryn Mawr Public Elementary School, later renamed Bouchet Math and Science Academy, teachers expected her to take after her brother. They would not be disappointed. "Without being immodest, we were always smart," Craig commented, "we were always driven, and we were always encouraged to do the best you can do, not just what's necessary."[16]

Michelle soon showed that she could be a little headstrong. Her parents had encouraged her to ask questions. As Marian said, "More important, even, than learning to read and write was to teach them to think. We told them,

'Make sure you respect your teachers, but don't hesitate to question them. Don't even allow us to just say anything to you. Ask us why.'"[17] Some of Michelle's teachers did not always appreciate this quality, and her parents soon heard about it. A friend of Michelle's from Harvard Law School stated, "I remember Michelle telling me about a teacher complaining about her temper in elementary school. She said her mom told the teacher, 'Yeah, she's got a temper. But we decided to keep her anyway!'"[18]

Whatever complaints her teachers might have had, they could not fault Michelle for her performance in the classroom. Though she did not like to take tests, this rarely affected her grades. "The academic part came first and early in our house," Craig remarked. "Our parents emphasized hard work and doing your best, and once you get trained like that, then you get used to it and you don't want to get anything but As and Bs."[19]

Just as Michelle did not hesitate to question her teachers, she would also speak up if her fellow students were acting up. "If somebody made noise in class, she'd whirl around and 'sssshhh' you," a Bryn Mawr classmate recalled. "If somebody was shoving somebody or being mean, she'd tell them to stop. Michelle always had a strong sense of what was right and wrong, and sometimes she'd be a tattletale."[20]

Like their parents, Craig and Michelle each skipped the second grade. In the sixth grade, Michelle was selected to participate in Bryn Mawr's gifted and talented program. This allowed her to take French and biology classes at Kennedy-King, a nearby junior college. In her biology class, Michelle and her fellow students would dissect rats and frogs. "This is not," a fellow student of Michelle's observed, "what normal seventh graders were getting."[21]

Though these new classes were difficult, Michelle rose to the challenge. "She didn't ever come home with grades that weren't the best," Marian remembered. "She always wanted to do her best, and I don't think it had anything to do with outdoing someone else. It's within her."[22]

There were other lessons that Michelle learned. While South Shore was a middle-class community and the Robinson household a stable and loving environment, the South Side as a whole had its rough edges that Michelle and Craig would have to live with. Michelle quickly grasped that her classroom achievements might please her and her family, but they could also lead to trouble in the schoolyard. Consequently, she developed the ability to, in her words, "speak two languages"—one with teachers, parents, and friends, and another with the rest of her fellow students. "If I'm not going to get my butt kicked every day after school," she reasoned, "I can't flaunt my intelligence in front of peers who are struggling with a whole range of things. . . . You've got to *be* smart without *acting* smart."[23]

Upon completing the eighth grade, Michelle graduated from Bryn Mawr. In a class of more than 100 students, Michelle was ranked second and served as salutatorian during the graduation ceremonies. Already she was showing the drive and determination of someone much older. It was a pattern she would repeat many times in the years ahead.

Whitney Young
High School

In 1964, the year Michelle Obama was born, the Civil Rights Act was passed by Congress and signed into law by President Lyndon B. Johnson. Four years later, the Fair Housing Act became law as well. The impact of these bills was far-reaching. Among other provisions, they outlawed racial discrimination in housing and education, and as time wore on, the system of segregation that existed in Chicago—and throughout the country—began to be dismantled. Whereas before, Fraser III had little choice but to join the corrupt Daley political machine to secure a better future for his family, his children could count on improved educational and employment opportunities.

The dismantling of segregation could be witnessed in the Robinsons' own South Shore neighborhood.

Unfortunately, it did not result in the integrated community for which many had hoped. The neighborhood was originally settled by German immigrants during the latter half of the nineteenth century. By the 1920s, Irish Catholics and Jewish immigrants had flocked to South Shore. In the 1950s, the neighborhood remained mostly white: Only one in a hundred residents was African American.

Over the next two decades, however, due in large measure to the Civil Rights Act, South Shore underwent a transformation. As blacks started to arrive in greater numbers, South Shore's white residents moved out. This was a common pattern throughout the country and was known as "white flight." Many whites feared that as blacks moved in, property values would plummet and city services dry up. Sadly, this often proved to be the case, and many realtors used these fears for their own profit, in a practice known as panic-peddling or blockbusting. These realtors would sell a house in a mostly white area to an African-American family, publicize the sale to the community, and then encourage other white residents to sell before the value of their homes declined, often offering to find them a house in the suburbs.

In South Shore, community organizations sprang up to keep white families from leaving. By 1980, however, South Shore was over 95 percent black. Unlike other urban areas, the process of "white flight" was civil in South Shore. Incidents of violence and angry words were rare, but the process did leave scars. As a neighbor of the Robinsons commented, "How do you think we felt? They [the white residents] were nice to our faces, but it was pretty clear we weren't good enough to live next to."[1] Still, the neighborhood maintained its middle-class character and did not experience the loss of businesses and services felt by other communities across the country

The Robinson family was aware of the changes that their neighborhood was experiencing and knew the role race played in bringing them about. As Craig said, "When you grow up as a black kid in a white world, so many times people are telling you, sometimes not maliciously, sometimes maliciously, you're not good enough." Thankfully both he and Michelle had the sort of parents who taught them not to let such feelings get them down. "To have a family, which we did, who constantly reminded you how smart you were, how good you were, how pleasant it was to be around you, how successful you could be, it's hard to combat. Our parents gave us a little head start by making us feel confident."[2] Michelle observed, "It was the greatest gift a child could receive, never doubting for a single minute that you're loved and cherished and have a place in this world."[3]

Though the Civil Rights Act enabled the desegregation of public schools, more than a decade after the bill was signed into law, a vast gulf in educational opportunities remained between black and white students in Chicago. The African-American community in Chicago had protested the situation for years. On the whole, schools with mostly black students were overcrowded, understaffed, and underfunded. Meanwhile, with many of the city's white residents moving to the suburbs, many mostly white schools were serving fewer and fewer students. The seemingly logical solution to these twin problems was to integrate the schools, but the city avoided this. Integration, it was thought, would only increase the rate of "white flight." So the city's black students remained bottled up in their second-rate schools, the overflow placed in portable classrooms. These trailers, made out of aluminum, became known as "Willis wagons,"[4] after school superintendent Benjamin Willis, and were widely resented by the black community, a symbol of the neglect with which it was treated by city government. Before long, the courts began to look into the slow pace of school integration in Chicago.

For the Robinsons, with their commitment to education, this situation meant that they needed to find other options for their children. Although there was a public high school only a block from their home, Michelle and Craig went elsewhere. As talented students, they wanted more than what was offered in their local community. Craig remembered, "We all wanted to go to the best schools we could."[5] Craig attended parochial school at Mount Carmel High, where he developed into a star on the basketball court. Michelle, as his biggest fan, would play the piano for him before big games to calm him down. As a spectator during close games, she often became so nervous that she had to walk out of the gymnasium.

A "GUTSY" CHOICE

Rather than go to parochial school like her brother, Michelle found another opportunity. In 1975, partly to comply with the courts on integrating city schools, but also to provide gifted and motivated African-American students like Michelle with the education they deserved, the Chicago Board of Education created the Whitney M. Young Magnet High School. As a magnet school, Whitney Young, which was located in Chicago's West Loop, would attract students from all over the city, not just those from the surrounding community. Named after Whitney Moore Young Jr., a civil rights leader from Kentucky, the school sought to attract a diverse student population and offer them the best education possible. Initially, the school's student body was supposed to be 40 percent white, 40 percent black, and 20 percent "other."[6] By the time Michelle started, however, the school was about 70 percent black, a pattern that continued after she graduated.

Unlike other mostly African-American schools, Whitney Young had fully equipped classrooms and laboratories, an Olympic-sized pool, and a radio station. Its students could

Michelle Obama, then Michelle Robinson, during her senior year at Whitney M. Young Magnet High School in 1981. While there, she was a popular student, who excelled at both her schoolwork and her extracurricular activities.

take honors courses and advanced placement (AP) classes for college credit. Whitney Young also had a partnership with the University of Illinois that allowed students to take college courses too.

Still, in order to attend Whitney Young and have access to all it offered, Michelle had to make some sacrifices. At the time, it was quite rare to leave one's own community to attend school, and Michelle had to get out of bed extra early if she wanted to be on time. She had to take a bus and the L, Chicago's famous elevated train. On average, the trip took an hour each way. On bad days, it could take up to two. Dagny Bloland, a teacher at Whitney Young, remarked:

> When [Michelle] applied and came here, the tradition of leaving one's neighborhood to go to high school was very new, and a person had to be gutsy to do it. For most kids who came here in those times, the idea that you would take two or three buses and a train to come here was a very new idea.[7]

EXCELLING AT SCHOOL

At Whitney Young, Michelle showed how much she valued her education. She made the honor roll every year and was inducted into the National Honor Society. Despite her good grades, Michelle continued to struggle with tests. But whatever she lacked in that department, she made up for with hard work and intense discipline. Unlike her brother, who according to Marian, "could pass a test just by carrying a book under his arm,"[8] Michelle had to study extra hard to measure up to the high standards she set for herself. Craig remembered, "I'd come home from basketball practice, and she'd be working. I'd sit down on the sofa and watch TV; she'd keep working. When I turned off the TV, she'd still be working."[9]

In the classroom, Michelle did not hesitate to challenge her teachers if she thought she was being treated unfairly. In a typing class, Michelle believed she had earned an A based on the number of words she typed in a minute. The teacher only gave her a B+. Michelle was relentless. "She badgered and badgered that teacher," Marian recollected. "I finally called her and told her, 'Michelle is not going to let this go.'"[10] Eventually, the teacher yielded and gave Michelle the A.

Michelle not only excelled in her academic work, she was also an accomplished pianist and practiced ballet, performing at school recitals. A popular student, she was active in student government as well, running successfully for student council and later for senior class treasurer, a contest she won by one vote. "Michelle was pretty much liked by everybody,"[11] a Whitney Young classmate observed. Michelle was especially close with Santita Jackson, daughter of the civil rights leader and presidential candidate Reverend Jesse Jackson, who recalled young Michelle Robinson as "an odds buster, and an overcomer. She always had her eye on the north star, so to speak."[12]

Along with the academic and extracurricular opportunities, Whitney Young offered Michelle a well-integrated, multiracial community, something that was hard to find outside the walls of the school. The secretary of Michelle's class, Michelle Ealey Toliver, stated:

> Although [Whitney Young] was racially diverse, the school was not racially divided. It was a melting pot. Our homecoming court was black and white, there was no racial undertone. Everything was just, I don't know, harmonious. Sports and everything. We had two Chinese guys who were phenomenal basketball players.[13]

The president of Michelle's class, Robert Mayfield, agreed: "It was racially diverse, it was ethnically diverse; it had great school spirit. It was pretty new, and it was fantastic."[14]

On top of her academic excellence, Michelle earned money babysitting and had an active social life. Her mother was shocked when she discovered that Michelle had bought herself a $300 Coach bag with her babysitting money. Michelle explained that the bag was well worth the price, telling her mother, "You're going to buy ten or twelve purses over the next few years, and all I need is this one."[15]

IVY LEAGUE ASPIRATIONS

As Michelle progressed through Whitney Young, her brother was completing his studies at Mount Carmel and thinking about where to go to college. With his skills on the basketball court and his good grades, he was highly recruited. Even though the University of Washington offered him a full scholarship, he had also been accepted at Princeton University, an Ivy League school and one of the best in the nation. Unfortunately, if he chose Princeton, he and his family would have to find a way to pay for it. Having worked so hard to instill the value of education in his children, Fraser III told Craig, "Go to the best school. Don't worry about the money. We'll find a way."[16] Still, Craig hesitated. His father, however, was all in favor of Princeton, and to persuade his son played his trump card, advising him, "If you pick a college based on how much I have to pay . . . I'll be very disappointed."[17] Craig chose Princeton.

After watching her brother get into Princeton, Michelle thought she might give it a try as well. "Princeton, the Ivy Leagues, swoop up kids like Craig," she commented. "A black kid from the South Side of Chicago that plays basketball and is smart. He was getting in everywhere. But I knew him, and I knew his study habits, and I was, like, 'I can do that, too.'"[18]

A guidance counselor at Whitney Young was not so sure, however, and informed Michelle that Princeton and her other top choice, Harvard, were not realistic. Her test scores, particularly her SATs, and her grades were not Ivy League caliber. This only increased Michelle's determination. "Every step of the way, there was somebody there telling me what I couldn't do," she recalled. "I applied to Princeton. 'You can't go there, your test scores aren't high enough.' I went."[19] She shared the same concerns about the financial burden her decision would place on her mother and father as her brother had had two years earlier. But she quickly overcame them. "My parents were always clear," she observed. "They always told us that you go to the best school and don't worry about money."[20]

Craig's tuition at Princeton then cost $14,000 per year. Fraser III's salary at the time was about $34,000. Consequently, to help pay for Craig's education, Marian went to work as an administrative assistant in a bank. To pay Michelle's way at Princeton, the family would need to take out student loans.

In 1981, Michelle graduated from Whitney Young, ranked thirty-second in her class. That September, she would follow her brother to Princeton, where Craig was already making quite an impression.

Princeton Blues

Michelle arrived in Princeton, New Jersey, in September 1981. For a young woman raised on the South Side of Chicago, Princeton University must have provided quite a culture shock. Of the more than 1,100 students in her class, Michelle was just one of only 94 African Americans. She noticed other things as well. While the South Side had its more well-off areas, Michelle could tell that many of her Princeton classmates came from privilege and were not afraid to show it. "I remember being shocked," Michelle recalled, "by students who drove BMWs. I didn't even know parents who drove BMWs."[1]

The racial divide at Princeton also had a big impact on Michelle's experience there. "I sometimes feel like a visitor on campus, as if I really don't belong," she later wrote in her senior thesis. "Regardless of the circumstances under which I interact with Whites at Princeton, it often seems as if, to them, I will always be Black first and a student second."[2]

An early incident in Michelle's Princeton career was especially telling. One of her two freshman-year roommates was a young woman from New Orleans, Louisiana, named Catherine Donnelly. Donnelly's mother was a hardworking single parent, who had made a number of sacrifices so that her daughter could attend Princeton. When she found out that Catherine was sharing a room with an African American, however, she called everyone she knew at Princeton, alumni and administration, to get a new dorm assignment. "I need to get my daughter's room changed right away," she told school housing officials. "We're from the South. We aren't used to living with black people."[3] No new room assignments were available, however. Upset, she called her own mother, Catherine's grandmother, who ordered her, "Take Catherine out of school *immediately*. Bring her home!"[4]

"Mom just blew a gasket when I described Michelle," Donnelly later recollected. "It was my secret shame."[5] Rather than return to New Orleans, she stayed and waited for another room to open up. Several months later, Donnelly moved to a new room and before long Michelle became just another face on campus. Michelle did not know the real reason for the room change until the story came to light during the 2008 presidential campaign. Reflecting on her relationship with Michelle, Donnelly admitted to having some regrets. "Michelle early on began to hang out with other black students," she remarked. "Princeton was just a very segregated place. I wish now that I had pushed harder

A photo of Blair Hall on the Princeton University campus in New Jersey. As an undergraduate at Princeton in the early 1980s, a young Michelle Robinson found it to be very segregated.

to be friends, but by the same token, she did not invite me to do things, either."[6]

Princeton, like the nation as a whole, was experiencing a complicated stage in racial relations. The progress of the civil rights era had given way to a period of white resentment and reaction, and few places illustrated this conflict more starkly than Princeton. As an institution, the school already had a checkered past, and for African-American students it was an issue that was all but impossible to avoid. As Lisa Rawlings, a black Princeton classmate of Michelle's, commented, "Definitely you got the feeling that you didn't belong. Like Michelle, it was my first experience with any kind of prejudice. I wasn't used to people asking me what my SAT scores were, with the implication that I didn't have the scores to get in, I didn't have the grades to get in."[7]

Princeton University had long had difficulties with race, even though during its early history in the late eighteenth century, several Native Americans and African Americans had studied at Princeton. Those facts were long forgotten by 1904, however, when Woodrow Wilson, the president of Princeton—and later of the United States—commented that "the whole temper and tradition of [Princeton] are such that no negro has ever applied for admission, and it seems extremely unlikely that the question will ever assume a practical form."[8]

A little over 30 years later, an African American, Bruce M. Wright, was accidentally accepted for admission. When Wright arrived on campus and Princeton officials found out that he was black, he was asked to leave. The reason, they informed him, was that given the number of white Southern students studying at the school, Wright might not feel welcome. Later, the dean of the chapel at Princeton gave Wright some advice: "The race problem is beyond solution in America. Don't waste your time fighting the system here."[9] Still, by the late 1940s, African Americans were graduating from Princeton, though not in very large numbers.

EATING CLUBS

While Princeton had been changing with the times, eventually admitting women and minorities, its old ways died hard. Throughout Princeton's history, social life revolved around eating clubs. More than just a place to dine, the eating clubs acted like fraternities and sororities and played a large role in determining who one's friends were on campus. To join an eating club, a prospective member would often go through the "bicker" process during which he or she would be aggressively questioned by club members.

After the interrogation, members would then debate whether or not to let in the prospect. During the 1950s, some eating clubs were notorious for not admitting Jews. After the school opened its admissions to women in 1969, three eating clubs limited their membership to males only, a situation that

RACE AT PRINCETON SINCE THE CIVIL RIGHTS MOVEMENT

As an outcome of the civil rights movement, affirmative action programs were instituted in many colleges and universities as well as in government and businesses. At Princeton University and other educational institutions, affirmative action sought to make up for centuries of discrimination against women and minorities by taking their disadvantaged status into account in admissions decisions. An added benefit of affirmative action in education, many believed, was the creation of a diverse student body: A school community composed of people from different races, backgrounds, and perspectives, it was thought, could only improve education for all.

Whatever its value, affirmative action led to a number of legal challenges brought by white applicants who felt they had been unfairly denied admission in favor of less-qualified minority candidates. In a 5–4 ruling, the U.S. Supreme Court declared in *Regents of the University of California v. Bakke* (1978), that racial quotas—reserving a particular number of seats in a class for minority students—were unconstitutional, but that race could be used as one of several factors in determining whom a school would admit.

lasted until the 1980s. As much as the eating clubs offered a social support network for members by giving them a built-in circle of friends, they also were exclusive, designed, for better or worse, to keep certain people out.

By the time Michelle came to Princeton, the "bicker" process had died out in many eating clubs where membership was determined by lottery. Still, some refused to admit

At Princeton and other colleges, the conflicts over affirmative action did not end with the Supreme Court ruling and continued to influence racial relations on campus. At Princeton, the problem was especially severe. In response to the school's decision to admit women in 1969, a small but prominent group called the Concerned Alumni of Princeton (CAP) soon emerged and challenged many of the changes taking place on campus, affirmative action among them. It was not only alumni making such noise. Vocal conservative groups at Princeton often set their sights on affirmative action programs, believing them to be as biased as the systems they were seeking to replace.

One irony of the battle over affirmative action at Princeton was that another form of preferential treatment took place that did not inspire the same outcry. At Princeton and other colleges, you were much more likely to be accepted if you were a legacy, or had a family member who had already attended. At Princeton in the mid-1980s, about 11 percent of each class was black or Hispanic. Legacies made 14 percent. Thanks to her brother, the future first lady was also a legacy.

women. In addition, the larger culture of the eating clubs that still reigned on campus often made minority students uncomfortable, and so they tended to avoid them.

THE THIRD WORLD CENTER

Michelle had no desire to apply to an eating club. Instead she took her meals in an inclusive cafeteria and student center called Stevenson Hall—what its members referred to as the "poor man's eating club."[10] Stevenson Hall was also equipped with a kosher kitchen where the school's Jewish students who were keeping kosher could prepare their meals. Most who used the kosher kitchen belonged to the Orthodox branch of the Jewish faith. Michelle and her girlfriends soon made friends with many of the Orthodox students. As her roommate and best friend Angela Acree recalled, "[We] did everything the Orthodox students did, which included going on a ski trip to Vermont with them one break."[11]

Michelle's social life revolved around the Third World Center. Established in 1971 by the university to serve its minority students, the Third World Center was located on Prospect Avenue and Olden Street. There, members could attend activities sponsored by the center, such as lectures and dances. For Michelle and other students of color, "The Third World Center was our life," Acree commented. "We hung out there, we partied there, we studied there."[12]

For its members, the Third World Center served as a much-needed alternative to the eating-club-dominated social life that held sway at Princeton. It also offered Michelle a second family. Accustomed to the untiring support of her parents, not to mention the familiar surroundings of South Shore and Whitney Young, Michelle found in the Third World Center a place at Princeton where she could feel at home. "We were each other's support system,"[13] Laurent Robinson-Brown, a Princeton classmate, declared.

Some found, especially in hindsight, that the center could also limit their social horizons. Michelle and Angela sometimes questioned the role it served at Princeton. Before their other classmates arrived on campus, for example, Princeton's black and Hispanic students were brought together for Third World Orientation Week. "We weren't sure whether they thought we needed an extra start or they just said, 'Let's bring all the black kids together,'"[14] Acree remarked. Given the racial climate on campus and the unique challenges the school's black and Latino students would face, that they might need extra support is understandable. Yet some found *all* the support they needed in the Third World Center and thus did not explore what else Princeton had to offer. Often pressure, real or imagined, developed so that students hesitated to branch out.

For minority students, finding one's way at Princeton without the Third World Center was not especially easy. Michelle and her best friends at Princeton, Acree and Suzanne Alele, often spoke of how white students they knew from class would pretend not to see them if they crossed paths on campus. Slights like these, whether intentional or not, made it difficult to leave one's comfort zone. Thankfully, the Third World Center made it possible for students of color to have a comfort zone at Princeton.

Deeply involved in the Third World Center throughout her time at Princeton, Michelle eventually served on its board. For a time she helped run the Third World Center's after-school program for the children of the university's food service and janitorial workers. One of the children, Jonathan Brasuell, still remembered Craig and Michelle fondly decades later and thought of them as an older brother and sister. Michelle often played the *Peanuts* theme for him on piano. "I could not go through a week," he recollected, "without hearing that."[15] Jonathan's mother, Czerny Brasuell, who was the director of the Third World Center, described Michelle as "one of the most empathetic people I have ever met, in her ability to feel what people were saying, her ability to understand."[16]

Michelle participated in the Black Thoughts Table and the Organization for Black Unity at the Third World Center. The former was a forum where participants could discuss racial issues. The Organization for Black Unity arranged speeches and other events for the benefit of the school's black community. With her tall and elegant frame, Michelle also modeled for two Third World Center–sponsored fashion shows: one to raise funds for famine victims in Ethiopia and the other for the after-school program.

AT WORK AND PLAY

For much of her time at Princeton, Michelle roomed with Angela Acree. As Acree recalled their living conditions, she remarked, "We were not rich. A lot of kids had TVs and sofas and chairs. We didn't. We couldn't afford any furniture, so we just had pillows on the floor, and a stereo."[17] Their room became a popular hangout for Princeton's African-American students. This was due in large measure to Michelle's record collection. Stevie Wonder, Luther Vandross, and Run-DMC could often be heard blaring from their stereo. Michelle also loved to shoot the breeze with her friends. She "giggled and laughed hysterically,"[18] Acree remembered.

Though she might have enjoyed spending time with her friends and at the Third World Center, Michelle did not allow these activities to interfere with her studies. As a sociology major with a minor in African-American studies, Michelle displayed the same focus and time-management skills she had mastered at Whitney Young. "She was not a procrastinator,"[19] Acree observed.

"JUST PRETEND YOU DON'T KNOW HER"

Two years ahead of Michelle at Princeton, Craig Robinson had found the school a difficult adjustment at first. After arriving in New York City from Chicago, he had taken a bus to Princeton carrying nothing with him but a suitcase and a duffel bag. "I was overwhelmed by Princeton," he later commented. "I was so far behind, and I didn't even have a fan."[20] During his first few months on campus, he worried about his performance. In need of a pep talk, he turned to his father, who gave him some useful advice. "He told me that you're not going to be number one at Princeton, but you're not going to be last either," Craig remembered. "That kind of put it all in perspective for me. After that, I was all right."[21] During his career at the school, he developed into one of the best basketball players that Princeton had ever seen.

Having his sister on campus did not make his life easier. Early on, Michelle voiced her displeasure with how French was taught at Princeton. "But you're teaching French all wrong," Michelle told a professor. "It's not conversational enough."[22] Embarrassed, Craig called his parents. "Mom," he said, "Michelle's here telling people they're not teaching French right." Having dealt with similar situations with her daughter in the past, Marian had some guidance for Craig: "Just pretend you don't know her."[23]

Being the sister of a school basketball star no doubt helped Michelle fit in at Princeton. Lisa Rawlings observed, "She knew a lot of people just because of him."[24] Still, Craig felt his presence may have hindered his sister in other ways. In particular, he thought he interfered with her dating. "I was in the way in a certain indirect way,"[25] he admitted. Michelle's romantic life had another problem: Michelle's impossibly high standards. "Dad again," Craig remarked. "No one could live up to him in her eyes."[26]

During his last two years at Princeton, Craig was named the Ivy League Player of the Year; he also led the division in field-goal percentage. After graduating in 1983, he entered the National Basketball Association (NBA) draft. He was selected by the Philadelphia 76ers in the fourth round, but never made the 76ers roster. He did, however, play two years of professional basketball in Great Britain.

PLANNING FOR THE FUTURE

During her senior year, Michelle had two major assignments: to apply to law school and to write her thesis. Becoming an attorney was something she had thought about for a long time. After her brother graduated, Michelle began thinking about her own post-Princeton career. As always, she made sure she was prepared.

During her junior year, she visited Princeton's career center where she found a list of Princeton graduates willing to give career guidance to students. She contacted Stephen Carlson, an attorney and partner at Sidley & Austin, a corporate law firm in Chicago, and asked for a summer job. Carlson could not help Michelle on that front but did give her the names of a number of Chicago-area legal aid organizations that often had work for college students, one of which gave Michelle a part-time summer job.

With that experience under her belt, Michelle set her sights on law school. She aimed high and persevered in spite of those who told her she was too ambitious. "I wanted to go to Harvard," she stated. "And that was 'probably a little too tough for me.' I didn't even know why they said that."[27] Harvard, like Princeton before it, proved the doubters wrong and offered Michelle admission. Once again, she worried about the cost. She already had student loans from Princeton and going to Harvard would put her in even more debt. Her father set her straight. "It would be foolish," he observed, "to get this far in your education and wind up going to a second-rate law school."[28] Michelle accepted Harvard's offer.

SENIOR THESIS

A thesis is a major research paper that many college students have to write in order to graduate. It serves, in many respects, as the culmination of their studies, drawing together all that they have learned as writers, researchers, and thinkers. Because her race had so influenced her life at Princeton and had given her minor in African-American studies, Michelle decided to make race the focus of her thesis. To gather material, Michelle sent out questionnaires to African-American Princeton alumni, asking them how their college experience had changed their views about themselves and their relationships with the black community and American society at large.

In many ways, Michelle's thesis, "Princeton-Educated Blacks and the Black Community," reflects her mixed feelings about her time at Princeton. On one hand, she describes the sense of alienation she experienced at the university. Many questionnaire respondents admitted to sharing similar misgivings. She also drew attention to Princeton's other race-related shortcomings. The school's African American studies program offered only four courses during her last semester, and Princeton had only five black professors with tenure.

Dealing with larger questions, Michelle observed that having attended such an elite institution, her career would likely take her deeper into the white-dominated world, the same one she did not feel a part of at Princeton. "The path I have chosen to follow by attending Princeton," she stated, "will likely lead to my further integration and/or assimilation into a White cultural and social structure that will only allow me to remain on the periphery of society; never becoming a full participant."[29]

Although ambivalent about this possibility, Michelle also felt a duty to use the options afforded her by Princeton to help her own community: "This realization has presently

Michelle Robinson (now Obama) poses for her college graduation photo at Princeton University in 1985. As her graduation loomed, she planned for her future at Harvard Law School.

made my goals to actively utilize my resources to benefit the Black community more desirable."[30] While her thesis would later serve as political ammunition for her husband's political opponents, who branded Michelle a racial separatist or worse, it was really a young woman's attempt to come to terms with where she fit in the African-American community and in the larger world.

As her law school adviser observed, "The question was whether I retain my identity given by my African-American parents, or whether the education from an elite university has transformed me into something different than what they made me."[31] The issue Michelle was dealing with was the choice between integration and segregation. Like the country as a whole, Michelle had discovered that integration was not easy. She also grasped that to realize her potential, to help her community, and to make the world a better place, she could not reject the opportunities she had been given.

Michelle dedicated her thesis to her family and the other people who had helped her grow into the woman she had become. "To Mom, Dad, Craig, and all of my special friends. Thank you for loving me and always making me feel good about myself."[32]

With her thesis and coursework complete, Michelle graduated cum laude—with honors—from Princeton as part of the class of 1985. With this stage of her life complete, Michelle looked ahead. That fall she left Chicago for Cambridge, Massachusetts, and Harvard Law School.

A Legal Career
Takes Shape

As Michelle took up her studies at one of the nation's most prestigious law schools, she encountered many of the same discouraging issues she had faced at Princeton. Again, the student body was largely white, wealthy, and privileged; the faculty mostly white men; and political and academic tension reigned on campus. Many assumed minority students had simply benefited from affirmative action. Michelle did not take the doubts about her abilities to heart. As her friend and fellow law student Verna Williams commented, Michelle "realized that she had been privileged by affirmative action, and she was very comfortable with that."[1] She had already grappled with the race issue at Princeton, and she wasn't going to let it get in her way. Charles J. Ogletree, Michelle's adviser at law school, remarked, "By the time she got to Harvard, she had answered the question. She could be both brilliant and black."[2] Whether inside or outside the classroom, Michelle would soon prove that she deserved to be at Harvard, that she was right where she belonged.

It was not an easy adjustment at first. Law school involves long hours and lots of hard work. Even for someone as gifted and driven as Michelle, it was difficult to keep up. Many times during her studies, she wondered if she had made the right choice. At one point she called Czerny Brasuell at the Third World Center and admitted, "If I could do this over, I'm not sure that I would."[3]

Whatever misgivings she may have had, Michelle did not let them interfere with her studies. She quickly made an impression on her classmates. "She had incredible presence," Verna Williams recalled. "She was very, very smart, very charismatic, very well spoken."[4] So good, in fact, that Williams asked Michelle to participate in a mock trial with her.

Her professors also could not help but notice her capabilities. David B. Wilkins, who taught a legal profession class, observed that many students avoid taking positions on tough issues. They prefer not to be pinned down or to be burdened with "the responsibilities of decision making," Wilkins commented. Michelle showed no such hesitation, Wilkins remembered; she "had no need for such fig leaves. She always stated her position clearly and decisively."[5]

Given the respect her professors and classmates had for her, Michelle could have pursued the traditional path of high-achieving law students and tried to "make" law review and become a contributor to the *Harvard Law Review*. For ambitious law students hoping to go on to prestigious judicial clerkships or other prominent positions, serving on the law review is an important step. Indeed, her future husband,

A photo of Harvard Law School's Langdell Hall. During the future first lady's time in law school, her professors marveled at her discipline and her willingness to take stands even on very controversial issues.

Barack Obama, would become the first African-American president of the *Harvard Law Review*. Michelle, however, had other priorities.

As she had at Princeton, Michelle joined a number of organizations dedicated to serving Harvard Law's black and minority students, including the Black Law Students Association and the *BlackLetter Law Journal*. The *BlackLetter Law Journal* provided an alternative to the traditional law review, focusing on minority issues. The Black Law Students Association, like the Third World Center at Princeton, served a valuable social function for Michelle and her fellow African-American students. It brought them together and gave them a forum where they could talk about an issue they had difficulty escaping—that of race. In these discussions, Michelle felt free to speak her mind, something she could not always do elsewhere. As a classmate observed, "She kept her feelings to herself most of the time, because she didn't want to be pigeonholed. . . . She didn't want to be defined solely by her race. Michelle had lots to say about lots of other things."[6]

LEGAL AID BUREAU

In addition to her class work, Michelle dedicated 20 hours each week to the Harvard Legal Aid Bureau. Housed in Gannett House, the same building as the *Harvard Law Review*, the Legal Aid Bureau had quite a different mission. The bureau's student volunteers offered free legal counsel to people from Boston, Cambridge, and the surrounding area who could not afford their own attorneys. Whether it was an evicted family challenging their landlord's decision or a poor couple trying to come to terms on a divorce, the Legal Aid Bureau would offer help. For those students like Michelle who were drawn to the law by a desire to make the world a better place, the Legal Aid Bureau was an excellent opportunity. Ronald Torbert, a classmate of Michelle's who worked at the Legal Aid Bureau, stated, "We got to do the kind of work we thought we came to law school eventually to do, but we were also working with real people."[7]

Coming from the South Side of Chicago, Michelle was far worldlier and less innocent than others at the Legal Aid Bureau. In her own neighborhood, she had witnessed poverty, desperation, governmental and societal neglect, and indifference. Some of her coworkers did not have the same experiences and were shocked by the grim situations they encountered. There were times when they became emotional or even cried, which exasperated Michelle.

Michelle brought the same commitment and diligence to her duties at the aid bureau as she did to her class work. "She was very mature, very bright," Torbert recalled. "She handled some of the more complex landlord-and-tenant issues. I just remember her being very serious about the work she did, and she really cared about the people she worked with."[8] Torbert added, "If there's one thing that stood out about her—she is not easily impressed. You think you're working hard, and I think her attitude is: 'Well, that's what you're supposed to do.'"[9]

THE FUTURE

Future lawyers are often motivated by a desire to use the law to change society for the better, to stand up for the poor and disadvantaged. At other times, they are after judicial clerkships and careers in the judiciary, politics, or government. The reality is that most who attend the top law schools end up joining corporate law firms, where they earn good money and can start paying back their loans. Public interest work, by comparison, tends to be hard to come by and is poorly paid. Consequently, although Michelle no doubt found her work for the Harvard Legal Aid Bureau the most fulfilling part of her Harvard career, she had to be realistic about her long-term choices.

Upon completing her second year at Harvard, Michelle accepted a summer position at Sidley & Austin in Chicago. Pleased with her work, Sidley & Austin, offered to hire her as an associate attorney in their Chicago office upon her graduation, with a starting salary of approximately $65,000 a year. Her father, who had worked for the water department her whole life, only made $40,000. With huge student loans, Michelle could not reject Sidley & Austin's offer. "The idea of making more money than both your parents combined ever made," Michelle observed, "is one you don't walk away from."[10] Upon finishing Harvard, she would return to Chicago and practice law for Sidley & Austin. "[She] would," Charles Ogletree commented, "navigate corporate America, but never forget her father's values or where she came from."

Michelle graduated as a member of Harvard Law School's class of 1988. In her class yearbook, family and friends of the students bought advertisements where they could leave personal messages for the graduates. Fraser III, Marian, and Craig took out an ad as well. Rather than the usual words of pride and congratulations, their note to Michelle read, "We knew you would do this fifteen years ago when we could never make you shut up."[11]

SIDLEY & AUSTIN

With her Harvard degree and Sidley & Austin job offer in hand, Michelle moved back into the small South Shore bungalow with her mom and dad. Soon after starting at Sidley & Austin, Michelle joined the firm's marketing, or intellectual property, division. Considered one of Sidley & Austin's more exciting departments, it handled the accounts for the boxing promoter Don King, Coors Beer, and Barney, the purple dinosaur whose PBS television program was a children's favorite, among others.

Michelle's boss at Sidley & Austin, Quincy White, described Michelle as "quite possibly the most ambitious associate I've every seen."[12] Early on in her time at Sidley & Austin, Michelle earned a demanding reputation. She was not afraid to request the most sought-after assignments. White tried to oblige her, giving her the Coors Beer account and other interesting work, but found that, "I couldn't give her something that would meet her sense of ambition to change the world."[13] Not one to quietly bide her time, Michelle sought out the most challenging work she could and was not afraid to step on toes in order to get what she wanted.

BARACK OBAMA

As Michelle dedicated herself to her career, her family worried that she would never meet someone to share her life with. She still lived at home and rarely dated. "She'd just fire these guys, one after the other," Craig commented. "It was brutal. Some of them were great guys, but they didn't stand a chance."[14]

In 1989, one of Michelle's Sidley & Austin colleagues asked her to mentor a first-year, African-American Harvard Law student who was spending the summer at the firm. It was rare for a first-year legal student to receive such a position; the spots were generally reserved for second-year students. Everyone was so taken with this individual, however, that they had made an exception. His name was Barack Obama.

"Barack Obama?" a skeptical Michelle asked. "What the hell kind of name is *Barack Obama*, anyway?"[15] The more she heard about him, the less impressed she was. When she found out he was from Hawaii, her doubts increased. She expected him to be "nerdy, strange, off-putting."[16] "He sounded too good to be true," she remarked. "I had dated a lot of brothers who had this kind of reputation coming in, so I figured he was one of those smooth brothers who could talk straight and impress people."[17]

Their earliest encounter was hardly a success. After being introduced, Barack and Michelle went out to lunch. Michelle noticed his ill-fitting sport coat and was taken aback by the cigarette in his mouth. Still, the two quickly developed a friendship, and it was not long before Barack asked her out on a date. Michelle replied, "No, nope. Very nice of you, but I'm not really interested in dating anybody right now."[18] Wary of how it would appear to coworkers, Michelle commented, "I thought, 'Now how would that look?' Here we are, the only two black people here, and we are dating? I'm thinking that looks pretty tacky."[19]

A circa-1991 photo of Barack Obama as a law student at Harvard University. When Michelle Robinson first met Barack Obama during her time working for the law firm Sidley & Austin, she put him off, believing she had no time for romantic distractions.

Barack did not take Michelle's repeated refusals to heart. He sent her flowers and notes, called her on the phone, and asked her out just about every day, although Michelle had told him that she had "no time for distractions—especially men."[20] Barack would not give up. He was smitten. Reflecting on their early courtship, he remembered "a glimmer that danced across her round, dark eyes whenever I looked at her, the slightest hint of uncertainty, as if, deep inside, she knew how fragile things were, and that if she ever let go, even for a moment, all her plans might quickly unravel. That touched me somehow, that trace of vulnerability."[21]

BARACK OBAMA

The forty-fourth president of the United States, Barack Hussein Obama, was born in Honolulu, Hawaii, on August 4, 1961, the son of 18-year-old Stanley Ann Dunham and Barack Hussein Obama Sr. Obama's mother was a white student originally from Wichita, Kansas. His father was from Kenya and was studying economics at the University of Hawaii on scholarship. Married in February 1961, Barack's parents separated in 1962 and divorced in 1964. During his early youth, Barack was often cared for by his maternal grandparents, Stanley and Madelyn Dunham.

His mother received a bachelor's degree in anthropology from the University of Hawaii in 1967. At about that time she married Lolo Soetoro, a fellow student originally from Indonesia. Soon after they married, they moved with Barack to Indonesia, settling in Jakarta. For the next four years, the young Barack attended local schools. In 1971, he returned to Hawaii to live with his grandparents, leaving behind his mother, stepfather, and half-sister, Maya.

Back in Hawaii, Barack attended the prestigious Punahou School from which he graduated in 1979. He then headed to Occidental College, in Los Angeles, California. After two years at Occidental, he transferred to Columbia University in New York City, graduating in 1983. He spent the next two years working in New York. In 1985, he moved to Chicago to begin a three-year stint as a community organizer on the South Side. In 1988, he applied and was accepted at Harvard Law School, taking up his studies there a year after Michelle had completed hers.

In vain, Michelle tried to set Barack up with a friend or two with no success. Though she refused to go out on a date with him, it was clear to others at Sidley & Austin that something was developing. Mary Carragher, who worked at the firm, recalled stopping by Michelle's office to find her and Barack lost in conversation. "I could tell by the body language, he's just courting her," Carragher commented. Rather than disrupt them, Carragher would say to herself, "You know what, I'm going back to my office."[22]

As she found out more about Obama, Michelle would amuse Carragher with the little facts that she had picked up, that he had a white mother from Kansas, for instance. Still, although it was obvious that Michelle was falling for him, she managed to conceal her interest. He was hard to resist. Yet Michelle put him off for months. "She was falling hard," Carragher remarked. "But always cool. I mean never, even when you'd see their interactions, she was not falling all over him. She was very cool."[23]

Slowly, Michelle began to relent. Barack managed to break down her reservations by taking her to a community meeting one Sunday morning in a church basement near the Altgeld Gardens housing project where he worked as an organizer before starting law school. Surrounded by African-American mothers who had known him for years, Barack was transformed in Michelle's eyes. "When he took off his jacket and rolled up his sleeves," Michelle remembered, "it was like seeing him for the first time." Barack gave a moving speech about "the world as it is and the world as it should be."[24] Michelle was touched. But still she would not go on a date. Finally, Barack offered to resign from the firm. Faced with this ultimatum, Michelle agreed to spend the day with him—if they did not call it a date.

On a sunny summer Saturday, Barack took Michelle to the Art Institute of Chicago, a famous museum. After lunch at one of the Art Institute's outdoor eateries, they walked to the movie theatre at Water Tower Place. There they saw *Do the Right Thing*, a film directed by Spike Lee about racial conflict in Brooklyn, New York. "So you see," Michelle commented, "there he was doing his cultural thing. He was pulling out all the stops."[25] While the two were waiting at the concession stand for popcorn, however, Michelle noticed someone from Sidley & Austin. Newton Minow, one of her superiors, was attending the film as well. Minow recalled the chance encounter fondly years later. They "were like a couple of teenagers, both obviously a little flustered that they'd been spotted together. It struck us as kind of sweet," he observed. "When you saw them it was obvious they belonged together."[26] After the film, Barack

IN HER OWN WORDS

In an interview, Michelle Obama reflected on her initial meeting with Barack Obama:

When there are people who are different from us, we automatically think, well, that's nothing like me and we have nothing in common. But we have more in common than not. His grandparents are very much midwestern, and in that respect, the midwestern value is: work hard, treat people with decency and respect, and do what you say you are going to do, your word is your bond. We're both worried about doing our best and doing the right thing.*

* Christopher Andersen, *Barack and Michelle: Portrait of an American Marriage.* New York: William Morrow, 2009, p. 127.

brought Michelle to the top of the John Hancock Building where they had cocktails and looked down on the city. "By the end of that date," Michelle said, "it was over. I was sold. He swept me off my feet."[27]

"NICE GUY. TOO BAD HE WON'T LAST."

Though Barack would have to return to Harvard at summer's end, he and Michelle knew they would stay together. A long-distance relationship was a big commitment. So big, in fact, that Michelle took Barack home to meet the family, one of the few men who had graduated to that important step. Barack observed, "It turned out that visiting the Robinson household was like dropping in on the set of *Leave It to Beaver*."[28] He was struck by how conventional, pleasant, and loving they all were, especially considering the challenges they faced. The Robinsons all liked Barack, though they did not expect to see much more of him. Craig commented, "He was very, very low-key. I loved the way he talked about his family because it was the way we talked about our family. I was thinking, 'Nice guy. Too bad he won't last.'"[29]

Whatever doubts Craig may have had about his sister's feelings for Barack, he knew it was serious when she asked him to play a game of pickup basketball with her new boyfriend and report back to her on what he discovered. Fraser III and Craig often spoke of how one could tell a great deal about a person's character by how he performed on the basketball court. Was he a ball hog? Was he afraid to shoot when the opportunity presented itself? Did he play dirty? Barack managed to pass this test. "Barack's game is just like his personality—he's confident, not afraid to shoot the ball when he's open. See, that says a lot about a guy," Craig declared. "A lot of guys wanna just be out there to say they were out there. But he wants to be out there and be a part of the game. He wants to try and win, and he wants to try and contribute."[30]

"Your boy is straight," he informed Michelle, "and he can ball."[31] Not long after this, Barack went back to Harvard, intent on becoming the first African American to head the *Harvard Law Review*. Michelle continued her career at Sidley & Austin. Before long, however, two tragedies would lead her to question the path she had chosen.

Tragedies and Turning Points

Though meeting Barack Obama had added something new and exciting to her life and led her to think about the possibility of marriage and family, Michelle went through some difficult times after she and Barack started dating. In early 1990, one of her best friends from Princeton, Suzanne Alele, came down with advanced lymphoma, a deadly form of cancer. Several months later, Michelle flew to the National Institutes of Health in Washington, D.C., to be with her dying friend. On June 23, 1990, with Michelle holding her hand, Alele passed away at the age of 25.

The tragedy led Michelle to reconsider some of the choices she had made. "I was confronted for the first time in my life with the fact that nothing was really guaranteed," she stated. "One of the things I remembered about Suzanne is she always made decisions that would make her happy and create a level of fulfillment. She was less concerned with pleasing other people, and thank God."[1]

Michelle began to wonder if the path Alele followed, one guided by the heart rather than the brain, might be the better course. Her career at Sidley & Austin, while challenging and well paid, did not make her happy. She wondered, "If *I* died in four months is this how I would have wanted to spend this time? Am I waking up every morning feeling excited about the work I'm doing? I need to figure out what I really love."[2]

As she wrestled with these questions, she reconsidered the role Princeton and Harvard Law had played in her life up until that point.

> I started thinking about the fact that I went to some of the best schools in the country and I have no idea what I want to do. That kind of stuff got me worked up because I thought, "This isn't education. You can make money and have a nice degree, but what are you learning about giving to the world, and finding your passion and letting that guide you?"[3]

Michelle wanted to give back to her community, to make a difference. She no longer felt Sidley & Austin, where she was on track to make partner, would give her the inner satisfaction that she needed. When she brought up the possibility of leaving her high-paying position, however, her friends and family were skeptical. "Don't you want to pay your student loans?"[4] her father asked.

Michelle also realized that if she and Barack were to have a future together, she could not count on him to make money. As president of the *Harvard Law Review*, he could have his pick of any legal job in the country, but he was set on writing a book and embarking on a political career, neither of which could be expected to pay well.

A DEATH IN THE FAMILY

Less than a year later, another tragedy struck that caused Michelle to truly take stock of her life. On March 6, 1991, Fraser III, as he did every morning, woke up early to get ready for work at the water plant. He had recently undergone kidney surgery and was in considerable pain. As he had always done, however, he gritted his teeth and tried to work through it. Unfortunately, the pain he was experiencing was not the kind to be ignored: It was the result of severe complications from his surgery.

Still, Fraser III climbed into his car and began the commute to the water plant. On his way there, at the age of 55, he passed away. "He died on his way to work," Michelle said. "He wasn't feeling well, but he was going to get in that car and go. That's how we grew up, living your life to be sure that you make the most of it. If what you're doing doesn't bring you joy every single day, what's the point?"[5]

With the passing of Fraser III, Barack flew to Chicago to be with Michelle for the funeral. "As the casket was lowered," he later wrote, "I promised Fraser Robinson that I would take care of his girl. I realized that in some unspoken, still tentative way, she and I were already becoming a family."[6]

ENGAGED

They had been dating for almost two years now, but when Michelle brought up the idea of marriage, Barack was quick to apply the brakes. Telling her marriage was just a formality, a scrap of paper, he tried to change the subject. It became an ongoing debate in their relationship, with Michelle pressuring him for a concrete commitment, and Barack doing his best to put her off.

As his Harvard Law graduation approached, Barack passed the Illinois bar exam, which allowed him to practice law in the state. To celebrate, he took Michelle out to dinner at Café Gordon, a famed Chicago eatery. Again, Michelle brought up the marriage question. Again, Barack shot her down. "Marriage, it doesn't mean anything," he told her. "It's really how you feel." An angry Michelle responded, "Look, buddy, I'm not one of these girls who'll just hang out forever. That's just not who I am."[7]

As she seethed, the waiter delivered her dessert plate, chocolate cake. Only it came with a velvet box containing a diamond engagement ring. Michelle was speechless. "That kind of shuts you up, doesn't it?"[8] Barack asked.

A NEW DIRECTION

As she and Barack looked ahead to their wedding and their life together, Michelle made a fateful decision. The deaths of her father and her friend had led her to a realization as to what she wanted out of her professional life. "I looked out at my neighborhood and sort of had an epiphany that I had to bring my skills to bear in the place that made me," she stated. "I wanted to have a career motivated by passion and not just money."[9] She left Sidley & Austin for a position in the Chicago mayor's office. Sidley & Austin was sorry to see her go.

In her new post, Michelle worked under Valerie Jarrett, a deputy chief of staff to Mayor Richard M. Daley, the son of the former mayor, Richard J. Daley. Given her father's role in the Daley machine of old, Michelle went into her initial interview with a number of doubts. Her meeting with Jarrett went so well, however, that these doubts were largely put to rest. For her part, Jarrett had dealt with the same issue Michelle was struggling with—whether to give up a high-paying career in favor of public service. She was so impressed with Michelle that she offered her the job on the spot. Before accepting, Michelle requested that Jarrett come to dinner with her and Barack. "My fiancé wants to know who is going to be looking out for me and making sure that I thrive,"[10] she said.

Michelle was not the only one skeptical of the younger Daley administration. Barack, who was now working on a voter registration drive, had his own hesitations, having often run up against the younger Daley machine during his time as a community organizer. Over dinner, Barack questioned Jarrett about the role Michelle would play in the administration and who would be looking out for her. Jarrett held up well. And with Barack's concerns addressed, Michelle went to work for the mayor.

She quickly impressed her coworkers. "You didn't go to her with a 311 problem," Jarrett remarked. "You went to her with a 911 problem, and she fixed it right away. She's that good."[11] Not long after Michelle was brought on board, Jarrett became the head of Chicago's Department of Planning and Development. Michelle followed her to the new department, taking up a post as the city's economic development coordinator. In her new position, Michelle helped promote projects to improve the city's economy and also hammered out contracts between the city and various businesses.

As a manager, Michelle had to deal with staffing issues. Sometimes individual employees were not performing their jobs well. It was up to Michelle to make sure they knew what their responsibilities were and to inform them when they were not holding up their end. Direct and to the point, Michelle handled this part of the job well. Many of her fellow managers were reluctant to scold or fire underperforming staff. Michelle, however, was not afraid to drop the ax if she thought it necessary. "I don't mind telling people what they need to know about their job performance," she commented. "If it's great, I'll let them know. If it's lousy, I'll let them know that, too."[12]

MEETING THE FUTURE IN-LAWS

Michelle was introduced to one side of Barack's family on a Christmas trip to Hawaii. Along with Barack's maternal grandparents, she also met his mother and half-sister, Maya.

VALERIE JARRETT

After serving as Michelle's boss during her time in the mayor's office and at the Department of Planning and Development, Valerie Jarrett and the Obamas remained close friends and confidants. She lent her support to Barack's blossoming political career, chairing the finance committee for his 2004 Senate campaign, among other efforts. She now serves in the White House as an assistant and special adviser to the president. The Obamas describe her as family.

It should come as no surprise that they grew so close. Jarrett and the Obamas have much in common. The daughter of James Edward Bowman, a renowned physician, and Barbara Taylor Bowman, a groundbreaking psychologist and researcher in early childhood education, Valerie Jarrett was born on November 14, 1956, in Shiraz, Iran, where her father was teaching. Like Barack, she had a far-flung childhood, living in Iran and England. Eventually the family returned to the United States and Chicago, where her father had first practiced medicine. The Bowmans lived on the South Side, in Hyde Park. James Bowman was the first African American to receive tenure in the University of Chicago's department of biological sciences. Jarrett attended the University of Chicago's well-regarded Laboratory Schools for her early education and graduated from the Northfield Mount Hermon School in Massachusetts in 1974. She went on to Stanford University, graduating in 1978, and earned her law degree from the University of Michigan in 1981.

Michelle quickly adapted to the Dunham's family rituals, among them hard-fought games of Scrabble and Christmas feasts of eggs, pancakes, and tropical fruit. The beauty and natural splendor of Hawaii appealed to Michelle, too.

Her education complete, Jarrett began a career in corporate law in Chicago. In 1983, she married Dr. William Jarrett, by whom she would have one daughter, Lauren. (The couple divorced in 1988.) Following the birth of her daughter, Jarrett wanted to do something that would make Lauren proud. So like Michelle, Jarrett left her high-paying position to serve in the mayor's office, joining the administration of Harold Washington, the first African American to lead the city. Following Washington's death and the election of Richard M. Daley, Jarrett signed on with the new mayor.

After Michelle's tenure with the city came to an end, Jarrett eventually headed the Chicago Transit Authority and the Chicago Stock Exchange. She left politics to serve as president and CEO of Habitat Company, a Chicago real-estate development firm. When Barack Obama became president, some speculated that his Senate seat might go to Jarrett. Her services were needed elsewhere, however. "I told her," Michelle said, "that I wanted her [in the White House], that it would give me a sense of comfort to know that [Barack] had somebody like her there by his side."*

---

* Jodi Kantor, "An Old Hometown Mentor, Still at Obama's Side," *New York Times*. November 23, 2008. http://www.nytimes.com/2008/11/24/us/politics/24jarrett.html?pagewanted=1&_r=2&hp.

Barack Obama and his wife, Michelle Robinson Obama, on their wedding day in 1992, with her mother, Marian Robinson (*left*), and his mother, Ann Dunham (*second from right*).

In the spring of 1992, Michelle traveled to Africa to meet the other side of Barack's family. The couple visited the small town of Alego, Kenya, on Lake Victoria, where many of Barack's half siblings, cousins, aunts, and uncles lived.

MARRIAGE

While Michelle was working for City Hall, Barack was registering voters for Project Vote ahead of the 1992 election.

Project Vote focused its efforts on Chicago's South Side, trying to convince more African Americans to become part of the democratic process. Project Vote was credited for helping Bill Clinton carry Illinois in the 1992 presidential election and aided the election of a new senator from Illinois, Carol Moseley-Braun, the first African-American woman ever to serve in the Senate. When not signing up voters, Barack worked on his memoir, *Dreams from My Father: A Story of Race and Inheritance.*

In October 1992, Barack and Michelle set their responsibilities aside to finally tie the knot. In a ceremony administered by Reverend Jeremiah Wright at Chicago's Trinity United Church of Christ, the two made their wedding vows. In attendance were some 130 guests. The reception was held at the South Shore Cultural Center, where Barack and Michelle danced to Nat King Cole's "Unforgettable." Michelle's childhood friend Santita Jackson also took the microphone for a time, belting out a Stevie Wonder song. For their honeymoon, Barack and Michelle went to California, where they drove the Pacific Coast Highway, a road that weaves through the mountains overlooking the Pacific Ocean.

Career, Politics, and Family

Back in Chicago, the couple lived for a time with Michelle's mother in her childhood home on South Euclid Avenue before purchasing a modest two-bedroom condo not far from the University of Chicago. Focused on building a career in politics, Barack served as a lecturer at the University of Chicago Law School starting in 1992. In 1993, he joined the civil rights law firm of Davis, Miner, Barnhill, & Galland. At the same time, he was working on his memoir.

None of these endeavors paid especially well, particularly considering the massive student loans that Barack and Michelle were carrying. Although she took a step down in pay to work for the city, Michelle did not let financial worries trouble her too much early in their marriage. She knew that the pursuit of wealth was not what moved her—or Barack. "His first car had so much rust that there was a rusted hole in the passenger door," she recalled. "You could see the ground when you were driving by. He loved that car. It would shake ferociously when it would start up. I thought, 'This brother is not interested in ever making a dime.' I would just have to love him for his values."[1]

PUBLIC ALLIES

After about a year and a half at the Department of Planning and Development, Michelle craved a new challenge. Barack had served as a founding board member of a new nonprofit organization (NPO) called Public Allies in the early 1990s. Public Allies prepared young people for careers in public service and nonprofit work by connecting them with volunteering opportunities. After opening a Chicago branch, Public Allies asked Barack to take the reins. Barack declined but suggested Michelle instead. In 1993, she took over the Chicago office.

For Michelle it meant another pay cut. It also involved a considerable leap of faith. Success was not assured, and she would not have anyone looking out for her as she had in her work for the city and for Sidley & Austin. "It sounded risky and just out there," Michelle later observed. "But for some reason it just spoke to me. This was the first time I said, 'This is what I say I care about. Right here. And I will have to run it.'"[2]

For the next three years, Michelle headed the Chicago office of Public Allies. Not only did she have to manage and expand a permanent office staff as well as a crew of volunteers, she also had to raise funds to keep the organization on a sound financial footing. At all these tasks, Michelle excelled. "You kind of know when you're in the presence of somebody who is really terrific," Jobi Petersen, who went through the

Public Allies program in Chicago, said of Michelle. "I owed a lot to her. She's really fair, she's calm, she's smart, and she's balanced and she's funny."[3] Julian Posada, Michelle's deputy director at Public Allies, observed, "There was an intensity to her that—you know, this has got to work, this is a big vision, this isn't easy. . . . Michelle's intensity was like: We have to deliver."[4] And deliver she did. Eventually, Public Allies became part of AmeriCorps, a government-sponsored community service initiative.

Much of the credit for the success of the Chicago branch of Public Allies belonged to Michelle. Years after she had moved on, her former coworkers still marveled at her contributions. She had laid a solid foundation for Public Allies, one that helped ensure the future success of the organization. As Paul Schmitz of Public Allies commented, "She built it to last."[5]

THE STATE SENATE

Following the publication of *Dreams from My Father* in the summer of 1995, Barack sought to launch his political career. While the book earned a positive reception from critics, it did not sell very well and did little to add to the young couple's financial security. A venture into politics at this point could only further hurt their wallets. But Barack saw an opportunity he could not pass up: State Senator Alice Palmer, who represented the Obamas' Hyde Park district in the Illinois legislature, announced she would not be running for reelection but would instead make a bid for the U.S. Congress. Barack decided to try for Palmer's seat.

Always skeptical of politics, Michelle tried to talk him out of it. "I was like, 'What are you talking about, politics, why on earth?'" she commented. "And of course I'm like, 'No, don't do it, we're just married, why would you want to do this?'"[6] If he won, the job would require Barack to spend much of his time in Springfield, the capital of Illinois, and a three-hour commute from Chicago. It was not so much that Michelle was against her husband's political ambitions; she just felt that the brand of state and local politics practiced in Illinois were not the best place for his talents. She wanted him to either make his name in national politics or to settle on a well-paid career. Yet he was determined to serve in the state senate. An exasperated Michelle could only go along with his plan, telling him, "I married you because you're cute and you're smart. But this is the dumbest thing you could have ever asked me to do."[7]

The campaign proved more eventful than most local races. After endorsing Obama as her successor, Palmer lost the Democratic primary for Congress. She then decided she wanted to return to the state senate. Barack, who had been campaigning for months, refused to bow out. In examining the signatures submitted by Palmer and his other opponents in order to get their names on the ballot, Barack's staff noted a number of irregularities. In the end, due to these irregularities, his opponents were removed from the ballot and he ran unopposed. After cruising to victory in the March 1996 Democratic primary, Barack's election in November was assured. He was sworn in to the state senate in January 1997.

THE HOME FRONT

Even when he had time to spare, Barack rarely did his share of the housework, leaving dishes in the sink, clothes on the floor, and dirty ashtrays strewn about his "Hole"—the small office he kept in their condo. Michelle often found herself cleaning up after him. Once he joined the state senate and began dividing his time between Chicago and Springfield, she sometimes saw him only on weekends. As they did when they were first dating, with Michelle in Chicago and Barack at law school at Harvard, they spent hours talking on the phone. But for Michelle, it was not enough, and she

admitted to feeling lonely during Barack's stays in Springfield. She also started to worry about their finances. They
had bills to pay and their salaries were not always enough
to cover their debts.

Adding to Michelle's unease was that they had been
trying for years without success to start a family. "When
it didn't happen right away," Marian Shields remarked,
"she got a little worried."[8] Finally, a doctor told Michelle
that stress might be keeping her from getting pregnant.
Working 60 hours a week at Public Allies, Michelle realized
the doctor had a point.

THE UNIVERSITY OF CHICAGO

If she was going to be a mother, Michelle felt she needed
a less demanding work schedule. She resigned from Public
Allies and took a part-time position at the University of
Chicago, serving as the associate dean of student services
and the first director of community relations and community services. As a product of the South Side, Michelle,
like many African Americans in the area, tended to view the
University of Chicago with a certain amount of suspicion.
In many ways, the University of Chicago was very much
like Princeton: one of the best educational institutions in
the country, but also at times a somewhat insular center of
wealth and privilege. Unlike Princeton, however, the University of Chicago was located in the middle of a dynamic,
working-class community, where it did not always seem like
a good fit.

"I grew up five minutes from the university and never
once went on campus," Michelle observed. "All the buildings have their backs to the community. The university
didn't think kids like me existed, and I certainly didn't
want anything to do with that place."[9] In her new position,
Michelle was charged with helping to change the university's relationship with its neighbors. She would connect

In order to spend more time with her family, Michelle Obama took a position at the University of Chicago and later the University of Chicago Hospitals, where she helped to connect these organizations with the surrounding community.

University of Chicago students with volunteer opportunities in the community and help break down the long-standing divisions between the school and the South Side.

MOTHERHOOD

In November 1997, Michelle got the news she had been waiting a long time to hear. She was finally pregnant. On July 4, 1998, she gave birth to Malia Ann Obama at the University of Chicago Medical Center. For the next three months, she and Barack bonded with their infant daughter. With the state legislature out of session and with Michelle on maternity leave from the University of Chicago, they finally had time to spend together.

When the summer ended, they both returned to work. Even with her mother and a babysitter to help out, Michelle had difficulty balancing her career and her responsibilities as a parent. Barack's long absences in Springfield did little to help. If the legislature was in session, Barack would be in the state capital from Tuesday through Thursday. When he was at home, he often had papers to grade or other work to attend to. This left Michelle to change the diapers and care for Malia, all while pursuing her own career. She would come home from work and find herself "very much alone. It was hard to suddenly be by yourself with a baby, and frankly I was angry,"[10] she remarked.

She started to feel like a single mother. When Barack was home, she left him long lists of chores to do and errands to run to make sure he contributed. Michelle shared her frustrations with her mother and brother. After a successful career on Wall Street, Craig had given it up to pursue his dream of coaching basketball. Now at Brown University, he tried, with his mother's assistance, to help Michelle. They had little success. "Barack seems to think he can just go out there and pursue his dreams," Michelle complained to her mother, "and leave all the heavy lifting around here to me."[11] "Michelle is really upset with Barack," Marian told Craig. "And you know she's not shy about telling him off."[12]

HIGHER OFFICE?

Though Michelle let her husband know how his career and personal habits were affecting the family, she was unable to dampen his political ambitions. In 1999, he decided to make a bid for the U.S. Congress, challenging Representative Bobby Rush in the 2000 Democratic primary. Bobby Rush was an experienced politician with strong ties to the community. As a former member of the Black Panthers and the Student Nonviolent Coordinating Committee (SNCC), he had made a name for himself both nationally and in the history books. While Rush had recently lost to Mayor Daley in the Chicago mayoral primary, few political observers felt that meant he was vulnerable to a primary challenge in his South Side congressional district. Barack thought he could beat him.

Michelle did not agree. "You are *so* wrong," she told him. "There is just no way that you are going to beat Bobby Rush."[13] She was right. In a campaign cursed with bad luck from the outset, Barack was soundly trounced by 31 points. Though she stood by him as he made his concession speech, Michelle knew the challenge was a bad idea from the start, one that would set back the family finances as well as Barack's political career. "When I launched my ill-fated congressional run, Michelle put up no pretense of being happy with the decision," Barack wrote in *The Audacity of Hope*. "Leaning down to kiss Michelle good-bye in the morning, all I would get was a peck on the cheek."[14]

After some difficult moments spent considering his political future, Barack returned to Springfield determined to continue his work and to prepare the ground for another bid at higher office, one that would remove the bitter taste left by his bruising primary defeat. "I am very competitive," Michelle observed, "but nothing like Barack. He is a terrible loser. It really gnaws away at him."[15]

NATASHA (SASHA)

Michelle continued to fret about the family finances. Though they were bringing in plenty of money, student loans, a mortgage, and campaign debt kept them from feeling secure. In the summer of 2000, for example, Barack flew to Los Angeles, California, to attend the Democratic National Convention. When he tried to rent a car, however, he found his credit card was maxed out.

That fall, Michelle discovered that she was again pregnant. While overjoyed at the prospect of becoming a mother for a second time, she worried about their financial security. She begged Barack to set aside his political goals and find better paying work. He told her not to worry, that everything would work out in time, but he returned to Springfield.

Natasha "Sasha" Obama was born on June 10, 2001. Once again, with the legislature out of session and Michelle on maternity leave, the family could enjoy a few months to themselves. Still it was a stressful time in Barack and Michelle's marriage. She resented Barack's absences and his lack of concern about money. And she felt the strain of caring for two young children largely by herself. Recalling those days, Barack stated in *The Audacity of Hope*, "My wife's anger toward me seemed barely contained. 'You only think about yourself,' she would tell me. 'I never thought I'd have to raise a family alone.'"[16]

In early September 2001, however, Sasha came down with meningitis, a potentially life-threatening illness. For three stressful days, Barack and Michelle camped out at the hospital as doctors struggled to save their infant daughter's life. A course of antibiotics helped Sasha fight off the infection, and in time she made a complete recovery. The experience was "a nightmare—the kind of thing you hope and pray will never happen to a child of yours," Michelle stated. "Any other parent would understand how desperate we felt, and how it brought us closer together."[17]

Then on September 11, 2001, terrorists from the al Qaeda network hijacked four commercial aircraft and crashed them into the Pentagon outside Washington, D.C.; the Twin Towers in New York City; and into a field in Pennsylvania. Nearly 3,000 people died in this coordinated terrorist attack. As it did for families in the United States and throughout the world, the tragedy of that day strengthened their bonds even further, cementing their commitment both to each other and to the nation. In the face of such horrors, their own disagreements now seemed small and insignificant.

As the days wore on, Michelle gained a new perspective on Barack, his ambitions, and how they fit into their family life. "I spent a lot of time expecting my husband to fix things," she commented. "But then I came to realize that he was there in the ways he could be. If he wasn't there, it didn't mean he wasn't a good father or didn't care. I saw it could be my mom or a great baby-sitter who helped. Once I was okay with that, my marriage got better."[18]

Reflecting on those months, she described them as "an important period of growth in our marriage. He was in the state senate, we had small kids, and it was hard. I was struggling with figuring out how to make it work for me."[19] And she did find ways to make it work. "This was an epiphany," she remarked. "I am sitting there with a new baby, angry, tired, and out of shape. The baby is up for that 4 o'clock feeding. And my husband is lying there, sleeping." Rather than take care of the the kids herself while he slept in, Michelle instead went for an early workout at her health club, leaving Barack to handle Sasha and Malia himself. "I would get home from the gym, and the girls would be up and fed," she recollected. "That was something I had to do for me."[20]

CAREER MOVES

Soon after Sasha's birth, Michelle made another career change. The University of Chicago Hospitals needed somebody to lead its community outreach efforts. Like the University of Chicago itself, the hospitals had mixed relations with the larger South Side. Given her success at building bridges between the university and the community, Michelle was recruited to do the same for the hospitals. For her initial interview, unable to find a babysitter, Michelle brought Sasha with her. "It was probably the most unique interview I've ever had,"[21] recalled University of Chicago Hospitals president Michael Riordan. Still, he was impressed, and Michelle accepted his job offer.

Michelle recruited volunteers from the South Side to help out at the medical centers. She also visited local health clinics to see what help they could use from the University of Chicago Hospitals. She would then send hospital volunteers to serve in these clinics. Throughout her efforts, she won the respect of all whom she worked with. "I have seen her in a meeting with the board of trustees giving a presentation," her supervisor Susan Sher commented. "I have seen her with angry patients and community residents. I have seen her talking down a two-year-old in the middle of a temper tantrum. She can handle them all."[22]

During this time, Barack had begun to think about the next step in his career. The attacks of September 11 had focused his mind on the problems confronting the nation and what he could do to help. After a great deal of soul-searching, he settled on a run for the United States Senate. He would seek to reclaim the seat once held by Carol

Moseley-Braun in the 2004 election. The current senator, Peter Fitzgerald, a Republican, was not especially popular in Illinois, and many thought he could face a challenge in the primary when he sought reelection. Barack felt he could win the Democratic primary and then the general election.

Michelle had her doubts. "The big issue around the Senate for me was, how on earth can we afford it?"[23] she commented. Even if he won, Michelle observed, their new life would be even more expensive, with homes in Chicago and Washington, D.C. How could they pay down their debts and save for college for Sasha and Malia? Barack told her he would just write another book. "Snake eyes there,"[24] Michelle responded. "Just write a book, yeah, that's right. Yep, yep, yep. And you'll climb the beanstalk and come back down with the golden egg, Jack."[25]

Whatever her concerns, Michelle had acquired some hard-earned wisdom regarding her husband and his aspirations. She knew running for the Senate was something he had to do. And she was not going to stand in his way. After he promised that if he failed in this bid, he would retire from politics, Michelle came onboard. "Whatever," she told him. "We'll figure it out. We're not hurting. Go ahead." Then, with a grin, she added, "Maybe you'll lose."[26]

HEADED FOR THE SENATE

In late 2002, Barack quietly started putting together his political team. Around the same time, the country was gearing up for war in Iraq. While public opinion throughout the country was largely in favor of launching the invasion, Barack was asked to speak to an antiwar rally in October. For an aspiring senator, to address such a crowd carried a number of risks. Still, Michelle encouraged Barack to participate. In his speech, citing the Civil War and World War II as justified wars, Barack stated that he was not opposed to all wars. "What I am opposed to is a dumb war," he remarked, "a rash war. A war based not on reason but on passion, not on principle but on politics."[27] As the months and years progressed and public opinion turned against the war in Iraq just as Barack's national profile grew, many voters, especially in the Democratic Party, recalled his early antiwar stand.

In April 2003, Senator Fitzgerald announced that he would not be running for reelection. The Democratic primary field swelled to nine candidates. Of these, Barack only worried about two: Dan Hynes, the state comptroller and early favorite Blair Hull, a former stock trader with deep pockets.

Michelle went out on the campaign trail to support her husband and quickly emerged as a powerful and charismatic voice, mixing a plainspoken, folksy appeal with a contagious idealism. She also brought her fund-raising skills to bear by using the network of contacts she had developed throughout her education and professional life to seek out donors to help support the campaign.

Toward the end of the primary season, Barack launched his first television ads using the slogan "Yes, we can." As Hull and Hynes hammered away at each other, Barack slowly built support. In the March 2004 primary, he won 53 percent of the vote, a shocking result. No African-American candidate had ever done so well. He had carried the black vote, the white suburban "collar" counties outside Chicago, and neighborhoods in northwestern Chicago that had never voted for a minority candidate. The unlikely coalition he built suggested that he was a new kind of politician, one who could transcend the ethnic politics that had long dominated the Democratic Party in Illinois. Whether he could extend that appeal beyond the base of the party to independents and Republicans would determine whether or not he would serve in the Senate.

The Republican candidate, Jack Ryan, appeared tough to beat. A good-looking millionaire with an Ivy League education, Ryan had given up a career on Wall Street to teach in inner-city schools. Ryan's campaign, however, self-destructed when his divorce proceedings unleashed a scandal that ended his political run. Ryan dropped out of the race on June 25, 2004.

To prevent Barack from running unopposed, the Republicans scrambled for a replacement candidate. Some suggested the former Chicago Bears head coach Mike Ditka might enter the race. Michelle worried that the beloved coach might just give Barack a run for his money.

As these events were playing themselves out, Senator John Kerry of Massachusetts, the Democratic Party's 2004 presidential nominee, was preparing for the national convention in Boston. Stuck in a tight race with President George W. Bush, Kerry needed someone to give a memorable keynote address on July 27. Kerry had met Barack at a June fund-raiser and was struck by his ability to connect with a crowd. Given the importance of the Senate seat in Illinois and Barack's gifts as a speaker, Kerry offered him the spot.

THE KEYNOTE ADDRESS

With Michelle's help, Barack started crafting his speech. When the Kerry campaign sought to edit it, Michelle told her husband, "Stick to your guns. You're the only one who knows what's right for you."[28] As the day of the speech approached, the tension built. The press had started buzzing about the unknown Barack Obama and the speech kept receiving edits and reedits. Finally, a frustrated Barack asked Michelle what she thought of it. "I think," she said, "that you're not going to embarrass the family."[29]

Before Barack went onstage to address the thousands in attendance at Boston's Fleet Center and the millions

The keynote address Barack Obama—then an Illinois state senator running for the U.S. Senate—delivered on the second night of the 2004 Democratic National Convention in Boston helped to cement his political career and made many party insiders suggest he someday run for president himself.

watching on television, Michelle made him change his tie from a red to a soft blue. She also gave one last piece of advice: "Just don't screw it up, buddy!"[30]

As she waited for her husband's moment, Michelle had some misgivings. She did not doubt his ability to deliver. Over the past several years, he had developed into a great orator. The speech he had written was a home run. She knew he would make the most of the moment and that, for their family, nothing would ever be the same. "I'm just kind of worried," Michelle admitted, "that things will never be normal again, you know?"[31]

Introduced by Senator Dick Durbin of Illinois, Barack Obama strode to the dais and delivered what most viewers and critics saw as a 17-minute masterpiece. He opened with his life story and what it said about the United States and the unlimited possibility the nation offered. He also called for national unity. "There's not a liberal America and a conservative America—there's a *United States* of America," he stated. "There's not a black America and a white America and a Latino America and an Asian America—there's the *United States* of America. . . . We are one people."[32] When he finished, the crowd roared its approval, and Michelle joined him onstage and waved to the cheering audience.

FROM BOSTON TO WASHINGTON

With his keynote address, Barack Obama had announced that a powerful new voice had emerged on the American stage. The pundits and the public were equally impressed. Returning to the campaign trail in Illinois, Barack was mobbed by supporters.

In August, the Republicans settled on a replacement for Ryan. Alan Keyes, a well-known commentator and past Republican presidential candidate, would take over. Like Barack, Keyes was African American and an eloquent speaker. His candidacy had some problems, however. He had never lived in Illinois, for one, and his take-no-prisoners style of speaking, while powerful, turned many voters off.

On November 2, 2004, Barack Obama overwhelmingly defeated Alan Keyes, winning 70 percent of the vote to Keyes' 26 percent. While exultant in victory, Barack and Michelle were disappointed with the presidential results: George W. Bush had narrowly defeated Kerry to win a second term. With the results barely in, journalists already started asking Barack if he planned on running for president in four years. He stated he would most definitely not be running. "I will hold you to that,"[33] Michelle told him.

On to the
White House

With Barack Obama a newly minted U.S. senator in January 2005, he and Michelle had to decide on their living arrangements. Thankfully, they no longer had to worry about money. His convention address had generated enough publicity to propel *Dreams from My Father* to the top of the best-seller lists. The money earned by the book allowed Barack and Michelle to finally pay off their school loans. And a follow-up to *Dreams* was already in the works.

Afraid of feeling lonely in Washington, Barack wanted Michelle, Malia, and Sasha to move there with him. Wary of upsetting the girls' education or their bond with their grandmother, Michelle vetoed that idea: "With all the crazy stuff going on, the best thing right now is not to disrupt their lives."[1] So Barack rented a small one-bedroom apartment in Washington, and Michelle and the girls stayed in Chicago.

With the campaign over, Michelle returned to full-time work at the University of Chicago Hospitals, earning a promotion to vice president and a hefty pay raise. With their improved finances, they purchased a six-bedroom house on the South Side, at the corner of East Hyde Park Boulevard and South Greenwood Drive. A friend of the Obamas, the Chicago developer Tony Rezko, helped arrange the deal. When Rezko was later indicted for financial misdealings, the Obamas were deeply embarrassed.

As was his habit during his time in Springfield, Barack would spend Tuesday through Thursday in Washington and then fly back to Chicago. While he was in the capital, Michelle kept him up-to-date on what the kids were doing. She also insisted that he arrange his schedule so that he could attend dance recitals, holiday festivities, and especially birthday parties. She also made sure they took their yearly family trip to Hawaii, where they saw Barack's ailing grandmother, who was sick with cancer.

PRESIDENTIAL TALK

Despite his claim that he was not interested in running for president in 2008, Barack Obama had captured much of the public's imagination. His important assignments in the Senate, his extensive travel schedule, and the crowds he drew at his every public appearance did not discourage such talk either. Meanwhile, in 2006 his second book, *The Audacity of Hope: Thoughts on Reclaiming the American Dream*, was released to positive reviews and quickly shot to the top of the best-seller lists. To promote the book, he and Michelle appeared on Oprah Winfrey's television show, raising the young senator's profile even further.

He and Michelle returned to Africa that summer and visited Kenya and a number of other countries, where they received an incredible reception, as adoring crowds numbering in the thousands greeted him. Though she had previously expressed doubts about Barack running for president, Michelle began to question her position when she saw the reaction he was inspiring. "[It] was very powerful," she commented at the time. "It's hard to interpret what all of this means to me and means to us."[2]

When asked by Tim Russert on the news program *Meet the Press* in October 2006 if he was going to run for president, the new senator did not say no. His advisers knew, however, that the only thing that could keep him from throwing his hat in the ring was Michelle. She had her doubts. She wondered if he would be able to raise enough money. There were already well-funded and well-known candidates in the race. She also worried whether a black candidate could win support nationally. A presidential campaign would disrupt their lives even further. His safety was a concern as well. She feared that a black man running for president could become a target.

Once again, the Obamas spent their 2006 Christmas holiday in Hawaii. There, Michelle and Barack discussed the presidential issue and her concerns. "I took myself down every dark road you could go on, just to prepare myself before we jumped out there," Michelle stated. "Are we emotionally, financially ready for this? I dreamed out all the scenarios."[3] Whatever her hesitations, she remarked, "they were addressed."[4] The next month, January 2007, Barack set up his presidential exploratory committee. "When you're in Hawaii, on a beach," Michelle later observed, "everything looks possible."[5]

AN ANNOUNCEMENT

In early February, Michelle took up a part-time post at the University of Chicago Hospitals. As it turned out, she would need the hours to campaign for her husband. On February 10, before a huge crowd at the Illinois state capitol in Springfield, Barack Obama announced his candidacy

Democratic presidential hopeful Barack Obama appears onstage with his wife, Michelle, and their daughters, Sasha and Malia, during his caucus night rally in Des Moines, Iowa, on January 3, 2008. His stunning victory in Iowa dealt a severe blow to the presidential ambitions of his rival for the Democratic nomination, Senator Hillary Rodham Clinton of New York.

for president. Michelle and the girls had managed to ring some concessions out of him. In exchange for Michelle's support, Barack had pledged to quit smoking. Sasha and Malia were promised a dog. "The way I look at it is, *we're* running for president of the United States. Me, Barack, Sasha, Malia, my mom, my brother, his sisters—we're all running," Michelle observed. "I can't hold down a full-time job as vice president of community and external affairs and be on the road three or four days a week."[6]

The Obamas hit the campaign trail hard. But Michelle made sure to arrange her schedule so that she would not miss any of Sasha's and Malia's recitals or sporting events. She also tried to be home every night to tuck them in. Thankfully, Michelle's mother retired in the summer of 2007 and helped out with the grandkids whenever she was needed. Michelle often found herself saying, "Thank God for Grandma!" Marian did not think the job a difficult one, however: "Michelle is such a disciplinarian," she noted, "there really isn't much for me to do."[7] So that the girls could still see their father each day, Michelle bought them Macintosh laptop computers so they could video chat with him. "It's harder for him, being on the road," Michelle commented. "I've got my girls and our routine. I am feeling their love. He is missing that."[8]

The early focus of the campaign was on Iowa, where the Iowa Caucuses would be held in January 2008. The Democratic field was shaping up into a three-person race between Obama, New York senator and former first lady Hillary Rodham Clinton, and John Edwards, a former North Carolina senator and the vice presidential nominee in 2004. Clinton had already acquired a number of important endorsements and had a large campaign fund to draw upon. Most assumed the nomination was hers to lose. The Obamas were not so sure.

VICTORY IN IOWA

On January 3, 2008, Barack Obama cruised to an historic victory in the Iowa Caucuses. Based on his momentum, most expected the nomination was now all but his. Clinton, however, managed to squeak out a win in their next showdown on January 8, the New Hampshire Primary. Without a clear front-runner, the two candidates dug in and prepared for a long nomination fight.

With the battle lines drawn, Michelle made one of her few missteps on the campaign trail. In a speech in Wisconsin in February, she said, "For the first time in my adult life I am proud of my country because it feels like hope is finally making a comeback."[9] Many of her husband's opponents saw in these remarks proof that Michelle was somehow anti-American. The comments were played repeatedly on cable news. Michelle regretted the negative attention and would not make the same mistake again.

As the campaign wore on, Michelle came under further attacks, particularly from the Fox News Channel, which has been criticized for having a conservative political bias to its news reporting. On one such occasion, a Fox News commentator characterized a fist bump exchanged by Barack and Michelle as a "terrorist fist jab."[10] Later on in the campaign, an Internet rumor surfaced alleging that there was a videotape of Michelle angrily uttering the word "whitey." Although there was no truth to it, the rumor mill had a life of its own and a way of shaping the public's view

IN HER OWN WORDS

During the 2008 presidential campaign, Michelle Obama found herself defending her patriotism on ABC's *The View*:

> I am proud of my country, without a doubt. I'm a girl who grew up in a working-class neighborhood in Chicago, and let me tell you, of course I'm proud. Nowhere but in America could my story be possible.*

* Christopher Andersen, *Barack and Michelle: Portrait of an American Marriage*, New York: William Morrow, 2009, p. 268.

of Michelle. *The National Review*, a politically conservative magazine, did not go easy either, putting her on the cover under the headline "Mrs. Grievance." Undaunted, Michelle took the lies and criticism in stride. Still, the issue of race was one that the campaign could not avoid, and Barack Obama would have to face it head-on if he was to make it to the White House.

THE WRIGHT CONTROVERSY

Jeremiah Wright, the Obamas' minister at Trinity United Church, had often made fiery sermons criticizing the United States and white America. Tapes of these sermons came to light in the middle of the primary campaign. Although neither of the Obamas had been present during these speeches, Wright's words threatened to tarnish Obama's candidacy. In response, the presidential candidate delivered a March 18 speech in Philadelphia entitled "A More Perfect Union." Michelle had offered her advice, telling him "you can't disown yourself from your family because they've got things wrong."[11] In "A More Perfect Union," he disavowed Wright's comments but not Wright himself. He also noted that his white grandmother had at times said things that could be perceived as offensive to blacks. He would not cut her off either. "These people are a part of me," he observed. "And they are a part of America, this country that I love."[12] Widely viewed as a success, the speech helped set Obama's candidacy back on track.

With the Wright controversy behind them, the Obamas forged ahead. Barack piled up the victories in a tough fight with Clinton. With his win in the North Carolina primary on May 6, he captured the necessary delegates to become the Democratic Party's nominee for president. "You did it," Michelle told him. "You did it."[13] Barack had become the first African-American presidential candidate from a major party in American history. Although it would be some time

REVEREND JEREMIAH WRIGHT

The controversial minister Jeremiah Alvesta Wright Jr. was born September 22, 1941, in Philadelphia, Pennsylvania, the son of a Baptist minister and a schoolteacher. After graduating from Central High School in 1959, he began college at Virginia Union University, in Richmond, Virginia. In 1961, he left his studies to join the U.S. Marine Corps. Two years later, he transferred from the Corps to the U.S. Navy, where he was trained as a medical technician. In 1966, he was part of a medical team that operated on President Lyndon Baines Johnson.

Following his discharge in 1967, Wright returned to college, completing his bachelor's and master's degrees in English from Howard University, in Washington, D.C. He later earned his master's of divinity from the University of Chicago Divinity School. In 1972, he became pastor of Trinity United Church of Christ in Chicago. He would lead Trinity for the next 36 years, until his retirement in 2008, building the church into one of the largest in the city. At Trinity, he would marry Barack and Michelle Obama, baptize Sasha and Malia, and with his phrase "the audacity to hope," inspire the title of the future president's second book, *The Audacity of Hope*.

Though Wright had served as a mentor and confidant to the Obamas, his controversial preaching led to their falling out. His sermons sometimes featured angry criticisms of the United States; in one, delivered shortly after the terrorist attacks of September 11, 2001, Wright drew a connection between the attacks and violence committed by the United States, like the dropping of atomic bombs on Hiroshima and Nagasaki, Japan, during World War II, or the brutality inflicted on Native Americans. Following Barack's "A More Perfect Union" speech, Wright's public comments became increasingly offensive, some of them anti-Semitic, leading the Obamas to sever the relationship completely.

Michelle Obama delivers a speech on day two of the 2008 Democratic National Convention. During her time on the campaign trail, she grew to be an assured and confident speaker.

before Clinton conceded, the Obamas geared up for the general election against the Republican candidate, Senator John McCain of Arizona.

Throughout the primary campaign, Michelle had shown she could connect with a crowd and serve as a superb stand-in for her husband. She knew the sort of struggles families were going through since the economy slid into a severe recession in late 2007. She also helped bring her husband down to earth, pointing out his flaws—his snoring, for example—so that the average voter could get a more complete picture of him as a man. Her sense of humor, however, often made the campaign staff nervous, and some commentators felt she could be rather insulting to her husband. Regardless, Michelle was not about to change. "I think I can only be who I can be in this role," she observed. "And that's going to come with all the plus[s] es and minuses and baggage and insecurities and all the things that I'll bring into it, plus my hopes and dreams along with it."[14]

THE GENERAL ELECTION

At the 2008 Democratic National Convention in Denver, Colorado, Michelle took the stage on August 25 to address the delegates and the millions watching throughout the nation. The occasion had added significance. That week 45 years earlier, the Reverend Martin Luther King Jr. had led the 1963 civil rights march on Washington, D.C., and delivered his famous "I Have a Dream" speech. Introduced by her brother, Craig, Michelle spoke of her upbringing and her family and the stakes of the upcoming election. She also spoke of her husband and the unique strengths he would bring to the White House. While Fraser III was not alive to witness his daughter's moment, Michelle made sure he was not forgotten:

> So tonight, in honor of my father's memory and my daughters' future—out of gratitude for those whose triumphs we mark this week, and those whose everyday sacrifices have brought us to this moment—let us devote ourselves to finishing their work; let us work together to fulfill their hopes; and let us stand together to elect Barack Obama president of the United States of America.[15]

With the convention complete and Senator Joe Biden of Delaware added to the ticket as the vice presidential candidate, the Obama campaign prepared for the general election. The Republican ticket of John McCain and Governor Sarah Palin of Alaska made a contest of it, but in September the economy, already sputtering, took a turn for the worse. The historic panic that followed, with Republican president George W. Bush in the White House, helped the Democrats. McCain and Palin questioned Obama's qualifications and his associations, but whatever doubts they raised did not diminish his lead in the polls. On Election Day, Obama won 365 votes in the Electoral College to McCain's 173 and won 52.9 percent of the popular vote to McCain's 45.7 percent. The United States of America had elected its first president with African ancestry and had forever changed Michelle Obama's life by making her its next first lady.

First Lady

After the historic presidential victory and the triumphant celebration in Grant Park, Michelle Obama had to shift gears quickly and prepare for the inauguration and the family's move to the White House. It was a huge undertaking. "You spend a year and a half running," Michelle explained to Barbara Walters, "and then they give you six weeks to change your life."[1] Even with all their new obligations, the Obamas could not back out of a holiday tradition and made sure to spend Christmas in Hawaii.

Among Michelle's first orders of business as first-lady-in-waiting was to make sure Malia and Sasha adjusted well to their new home. "My first job in all honesty is going to continue to be mom-in-chief," Michelle commented, "making sure that in this transition, which will be even more of a transition for the girls . . . that they are settled and that they know they will continue to be the center of our universe."2 Michelle and Barack invited Michelle's mother, Marian, to come to the White House to live with them and help care for the girls. Michelle also appreciated the advice Hillary Clinton gave her. The former first lady told Michelle to make sure the girls had as normal a life as possible, that they cleaned up after themselves, and that the White House staff did not spoil them. For their education, Michelle and Barack decided to send the girls to Sidwell Friends, a well-regarded private school in Washington, D.C.

As her husband set about planning the inauguration, recruiting staff to serve in his administration, and constructing his first-term agenda, Michelle arranged the move to 1600 Pennsylvania Avenue. By and large, she did not bring much from their house in Chicago. They decided to leave their South Side home unchanged so they could return there for regular visits.

THE INAUGURATION

On January 20, 2009, Washington, D.C., was overrun with visitors who had traveled from across the nation to see Barack Obama's inauguration. The crowd was estimated at a million, the largest in history, a large portion of whom were African Americans who had come to witness the swearing-in of the first black president in the country's history. As Barack took the oath of office, Michelle, in a creamy yellow outfit, held the Bible upon which he rested his hand.

Following the inaugural address, the Obamas had a slew of festivities to attend. During the inaugural parade to the White House, Barack and Michelle left their limousine to walk down Pennsylvania Avenue, waving to the crowd, as has been tradition. That evening they attended no less than 10 inaugural balls. Michelle wore a white dress designed by

Chief Justice John G. Roberts Jr. (*right*) administers the presidential oath of office to Barack Obama (*left*) on January 20, 2009. Holding the Bible is his wife, Michelle, as their daughters, Malia and Sasha, look on.

Jason Wu. For Barack and Michelle's first dance as president and first lady, the song "At Last," by Etta James, was played.

With the inaugural celebrations complete, the Obamas set about fulfilling their duties as president and first lady. Given the tough economic times, Michelle turned down the $100,000 stipend to redecorate the White House living quarters, opting to pay for any renovations out of their own pockets. She also set some ground rules for Sasha and Malia. On most nights they have to be in bed by 8 o'clock. They likewise must make their own beds in the morning and do other chores. But it is not all structure and responsibility for the Obama daughters. In addition to Bo, the Portuguese Water Dog that was their reward for their father's presidential campaign, they received a swing set, which was installed on the White House grounds.

HEALTHY EATING AND FIGHTING OBESITY

As one of her first official projects, Michelle organized the planting of the White House kitchen garden on the South Lawn. It was the first garden at the White House since World War II, when Eleanor Roosevelt started one as part of the war effort. The produce grown in the garden is used in the White House kitchen or donated to local shelters. The main purpose of the garden, the first lady explained, is to educate young people about the benefits of a healthy diet.

Taking on childhood obesity is another one of Michelle's major efforts as first lady. In 2010, she launched the "Let's Move" initiative to encourage regular exercise and healthy eating. "The whole goal of this initiative," Michelle remarked, "is to end the problem of childhood obesity in a generation. We want kids born today to grow up at a healthy weight."[3]

STANDING UP FOR MILITARY FAMILIES

Along with her work on health and nutrition, the first lady has focused on several other important issues. She has made regular visits to military families and has sought to bring attention to the often-difficult circumstances they must contend with. She made the rounds of the military bases and hospitals to better understand the concerns of the men and women of the armed forces and their loved ones. In January 2010, she announced new federal funding dedicated to helping military families. These funds "are the result of military families speaking up and being heard," she declared. "And they are part of a larger ongoing commit-

First Lady Michelle Obama works in her vegetable garden, the first planted at the White House since Eleanor Roosevelt's era. Obama planted the garden as part of her efforts to combat childhood obesity.

ment to care for our troops and their families even after the fighting ends."[4]

Michelle has sought to address work-family balance as well. Throughout her life, she has noticed that work is taking up more and more of people's time. In her own family, she was lucky to have a stay-at-home mom. Nowadays, however, most families need two sources of income to make ends meet. With both parents working, there is less time to spend together as a family. As a mother herself, Michelle had difficulty attending to her various personal and professional responsibilities. As first lady, or "mom-in-chief," she has called on American employers to adopt policies that help workers better arrange their professional and family obligations.

HAITIAN RELIEF

After a devastating earthquake in January 2010 killed hundreds of thousands in the Caribbean nation of Haiti and reduced much of the impoverished nation to rubble, the first lady took the lead in raising money for Haitian relief. She issued a televised plea calling for donations toward helping the country rebuild. In April 2010, she made an unannounced visit to Haiti to view recovery efforts and draw further attention to the plight of the Haitian people.

President Obama's first two years in the White House were eventful ones. Among other achievements, he passed an economic stimulus package, signed historic national health-care legislation into law, and won the Nobel Peace Prize. Nevertheless, his standing with the American people took some hits. Michelle, however, grew in popularity, boasting some of the highest approval ratings ever enjoyed by a first lady. Her early service was not flawless, of course. During a visit to Great Britain in the spring of 2009, she made headlines for putting her arm around Queen Elizabeth II, which according to the rules of etiquette, is not permitted. The queen, however, did not take offense. Then, in October 2009, Michelle made a heartfelt appeal to the International Olympic Committee in hopes of landing the 2016 Summer Games for her hometown of Chicago. She even flew to Copenhagen, Denmark, to make her case in person. Unfortunately the committee was not swayed by her televised speech and instead chose Rio de Janeiro as the host city.

(continues on page 120)

JACQUELINE KENNEDY

For her grace, style, and beauty—and, in her mid-forties, her comparative youth—Michelle Obama is often compared to another first lady, Jackie Kennedy, the wife of President John F. Kennedy. Born Jacqueline Bouvier on July 28, 1929, in Southampton, New York, Jackie had a much more privileged upbringing than Michelle. Her father, John "Jack" Bouvier was a wealthy stockbroker; her mother, the former Janet Norton Lee, came from a rich society family.

On May 31, 1961, First Lady Jacqueline Kennedy and President John F. Kennedy leave the Quai D'Orsay ministry for the Élysée Palace in Paris, France.

For her early education, Jackie attended elite private schools in New York City and Washington, D.C. Her family life was often difficult, however, and in 1942 her parents divorced and her mother soon remarried. Jackie graduated from Miss Porter's School, a boarding school in Farmington, Connecticut, and went on to Vassar College in Poughkeepsie, New York. After two years at Vassar, she spent her junior year studying at the

Sorbonne in Paris, France, before graduating in 1949 from George Washington University with a B.A. in French literature.

A gifted writer, Jackie won *Vogue*'s Prix de Paris contest and authored features for the *Washington Times-Herald*. On September 12, 1953, she married Kennedy, then a senator from Massachusetts, at St. Mary's Church in Newport, Rhode Island. Their first child, Caroline, was born November 27, 1957. Their second, John F. Kennedy Jr., was born not long after his father was elected president, on November 25, 1960.

As first lady, Jackie championed the arts and took charge of redecorating the White House, hosting a television special to highlight her work. These efforts, though significant, were eclipsed by her hold on the public imagination, as she quickly grew into a major figure in fashion and culture. She was with her husband when he was assassinated in Dallas, Texas, on November 22, 1963, stood by his successor, Lyndon Johnson, as he took the oath of office, and planned her martyred husband's state funeral.

After leaving the White House, Jackie helped organize the John F. Kennedy Presidential Library. Her first priority, however, was always her children, whose privacy she went to great lengths to guard. In 1968, she married Aristotle Onassis, a wealthy Greek industrialist. The couple split their time between Greece and Paris. Following Aristotle's death in 1975, Jackie returned to New York City, where she worked as an editor in book publishing. She maintained her commitment to the arts throughout her life, among other initiatives, leading a campaign to save New York's neo-classical Grand Central Station from demolition. She passed away on May 19, 1994.

(continued from page 117)

"FIRST LADY OF FASHION"

Along with her widespread popularity, Michelle also received praise for her style, developing into something of a fashion icon. Many noted her sharp wardrobe during the presidential campaign, but once she took up residence at the White House even more attention was paid to her fashion choices. Soon books dedicated to her fashion sense were being published.

With her tall frame and toned physique, Michelle wears clothes well and has earned raves for her wardrobe selections. She tends to mix modest off-the-rack attire with more high-end, designer creations. In March 2009 she appeared on the cover of *Vogue* magazine, securing her place as one of the country's major trendsetters and the most stylish first lady since Jackie Kennedy.

WHITE HOUSE SCHEDULES

As first lady, Michelle Obama begins her day early. She rises at about 4:30 A.M., walks the dog, and tries to fit in a morning workout. She also helps Sasha and Malia prepare for school. By 10 A.M., she goes to her own office in the East Wing of the White House, where she usually works until about 3 or 4 P.M., when the girls return from school. During the day, she stops by and visits her husband in the Oval Office or he comes to see her. In the evening, she helps her daughters with their homework and serves as White House hostess. At family dinners, the Obamas often play a game called Roses and Thorns, during which they each describe the best and worst thing that happened to them in the course of their day. After tucking in Sasha and Malia at 8 P.M., Michelle and Barack usually go to sleep at about 10 P.M.

In keeping with her view of the White House as "the people's house," Michelle often opens her home to the surrounding community, inviting local schoolchildren in for visits. She also tries to get out into Washington, D.C., as frequently as possible to show their neighbors that the first family is engaging with the city and its residents.

During the 2008 campaign, Michelle visited a beauty parlor in a small South Carolina town. A 10-year-old African-American girl she met there described what it would mean to her if Barack Obama won the White House. "It means," the girl said, "I can imagine *anything* for myself." This struck a chord with Michelle. The little girl, Michelle thought, "could have been me. Because the truth is, I'm not supposed to be here."[5] But as a career woman, wife, mother, and now as first lady, Michelle never listened to those who told her she could not do something. She worked hard and followed her dreams, climbing higher than anyone could have expected, rising from the small South Shore bungalow all the way to the White House. Her life stands as a powerful tribute to American possibility—and what faith and sacrifice can accomplish. "Hold on to the hope that brought you today," the first lady has said, "the hope of laborers and immigrants, settlers and slaves."[6]

CHRONOLOGY

1964   Born Michelle Robinson on January 17, in Chicago, Illinois, the daughter of Fraser Robinson III and Marian Shields.

1970   Begins grade school at Bryn Mawr Elementary.

1977   Graduates from Bryn Mawr Elementary ranked second in her class; starts high school at Whitney M. Young High School.

1981   Graduates from Whitney M. Young High School; enters Princeton University.

1985   Graduates from Princeton with a degree in sociology and a minor in African-American studies; begins Harvard Law School.

1988   Completes Harvard Law School; returns to Chicago to work at the law firm of Sidley & Austin.

1989   Meets Barack Obama at Sidley & Austin in June; the two begin dating later that summer.

1990   Michelle's friend Suzanne Alele passes away from cancer on June 23.

1991   Michelle's father, Fraser III, passes away on March 6 at the age of 55; Michelle and Barack are engaged; Michelle leaves Sidley & Austin for a post in the office of Richard M. Daley, the mayor of Chicago.

1992   Marries Barack Obama on October 19, in Chicago, Illinois; leaves the mayor's office for a position as assistant commissioner at the Chicago department of planning and development.

1993   Starts a new job as the founding director of the Chicago branch of the Public Allies nonprofit organization.

1996	Takes up a position as associate dean of student services at the University of Chicago; Barack elected to Illinois state senate on November 5.
1998	Gives birth to her daughter, Malia Ann Obama, on July 4.
1999	Against Michelle's advice, Barack launches a bid for the U.S. House of Representatives in September, challenging Representative Bobby Rush in the Democratic primary.
2000	Barack is soundly defeated by Bobby Rush in the Democratic primary.
2001	Barack and Michelle's second daughter, Natasha (Sasha) Obama, is born on June 10; Michelle leaves her post at the University of Chicago to serve as executive director of community and external affairs at the University of Chicago Hospitals.
2003	Barack announces bid for the U.S. Senate in January.
2004	Barack wins the Democratic primary in March; delivers the keynote address at the Democratic National Convention on July 27; wins election to the U.S. Senate on November 2.
2005	Barack is sworn into the U.S. Senate on January 4; Michelle is promoted to vice president of community and external affairs at the University of Chicago Hospitals.
2007	Barack announces his presidential campaign on February 10; Michelle takes a leave from her job to focus on the presidential campaign.

2008 Addresses Democratic National Convention on August 25; Barack accepts the Democratic presidential nomination on August 27; he wins the presidential election, defeating Republican John McCain, on November 4.

2009 On January 20, Barack is sworn in as president; Michelle becomes first lady; the Obamas and Michelle's mother move into the White House.

2010 In April, Michelle Obama visits Haiti as first lady, to view recovery efforts following a devastating earthquake.

NOTES

CHAPTER 1

1. Christopher Andersen, *Barack and Michelle: Portrait of an American Marriage*. New York: William Morrow, 2009, p. 280.
2. Ibid., p. 281.
3. Transcript of Barack Obama's Victory Speech, National Public Radio. November 5, 2008. http://www.npr.org/templates/story/story.php?storyId=96624326.
4. Ibid.
5. Transcript of Michelle Obama's Convention Speech, National Public Radio. August 25, 2008. http://www.npr.org/templates/story/story.php?storyId=93963863.

CHAPTER 2

1. Shailagh Murray, "A Family Tree Rooted in American Soil," *Washington Post*. October 2, 2008. http://www.washingtonpost.com/wp-dyn/content/story/2008/10/01/ST2008100103245.html.
2. David Colbert, *Michelle Obama: An American Story*. Boston: Houghton Mifflin, Harcourt, 2009, p. 29.
3. Rachel L. Swarns and Jodi Kantor, "In First Lady's Roots, a Complex Path From Slavery," *New York Times*. October 7, 2009. http://www.nytimes.com/2009/10/08/us/politics/08genealogy.html.
4. Ibid.
5. Colbert, *Michelle Obama*, pp. 48–49.

CHAPTER 3

1. Liza Mundy, *Michelle: A Biography*. New York: Simon & Schuster, 2008, p. 1.
2. Colbert, *Michelle Obama*, pp. 10–11.

3. Ibid., p. 12.

4. Ibid., p.14.

5. David Bergen Brophy, *Michelle Obama: Meet the First Lady*. New York: Harper Collins, 2009, p. 8.

6. Colbert, *Michelle Obama*, p. 15.

7. Ibid., p. 16.

8. Ibid., p. 18.

9. Brophy, *Michelle Obama*, p. 13.

10. Andersen, *Barack and Michelle*, p. 80.

11. Brophy, *Michelle Obama*, p. 11.

12. Ibid.

13. Andersen, *Barack and Michelle*, p. 79.

14. Colbert, *Michelle Obama*, p. 21.

15. Andersen, *Barack and Michelle*, p. 79.

16. Brophy, *Michelle Obama*, p. 17.

17. Ibid., p. 18.

18. Ibid., p. 19.

19. Colbert, *Michelle Obama*, p. 22.

20. Andersen, *Barack and Michelle*, pp. 82–83.

21. Brophy, *Michelle Obama*, pp. 19–20.

22. Andersen, *Barack and Michelle*, p. 81.

23. Ibid., p. 83.

CHAPTER 4

1. Andersen, *Barack and Michelle*, p. 77.

2. Mundy, *Michelle*, p. 37.

3. Colbert, *Michelle Obama*, p. 17.

4. Mundy, *Michelle*, p. 45.

5. Brophy, *Michelle Obama*, p. 17.

6. Ibid., p. 84.

7. Mundy, *Michelle*, pp. 50–51.

8. Ibid., p. 57.

9. Brophy, *Michelle Obama*, p. 25.

10. Colbert, *Michelle Obama*, p. 55.

11. Andersen, *Barack and Michelle*, p. 85.
12. Mundy, *Michelle*, p. 56.
13. Ibid., p. 55.
14. Colbert, *Michelle Obama*, p. 57.
15. Andersen, *Barack and Michelle*, p. 88.
16. Ibid.
17. Colbert, *Michelle Obama*, p. 64.
18. Andersen, *Barack and Michelle*, p. 88.
19. Mundy, *Michelle*, p. 58.
20. Ibid., p. 59.

CHAPTER 5

1. Brophy, *Michelle Obama*, p. 29.
2. Colbert, *Michelle Obama*, p. 81.
3. Andersen, *Barack and Michelle*, p. 70.
4. Ibid.
5. Mundy, *Michelle*, p. 67.
6. Andersen, *Barack and Michelle*, p. 71.
7. Mundy, *Michelle*, p. 79.
8. Ibid., p. 61.
9. Ibid., p. 62.
10. Ibid., p. 71.
11. Colbert, *Michelle Obama*, p. 78.
12. Andersen, *Barack and Michelle*, p. 90.
13. Ibid.
14. Colbert, *Michelle Obama*, p. 82.
15. Andersen, *Barack and Michelle*, p. 90.
16. Mundy, *Michelle*, p. 72.
17. Andersen, *Barack and Michelle*, p. 92.
18. Ibid.
19. Ibid.
20. Mundy, *Michelle*, p. 59.
21. Ibid.
22. Andersen, *Barack and Michelle*, p. 91.

23. Colbert, *Michelle Obama*, p. 76.
24. Mundy, *Michelle*, p. 79.
25. Mundy, *Michelle*, p. 73.
26. Andersen, *Barack and Michelle*, p. 93.
27. Mundy, *Michelle*, p. 58.
28. Andersen, *Barack and Michelle*, p. 94.
29. Mundy, *Michelle*, p. 74.
30. Ibid.
31. Ibid., p. 77.
32. Brophy, *Michelle Obama*, p. 31.

CHAPTER 6

1. Andersen, *Barack and Michelle*, p. 95.
2. Brophy, *Michelle Obama*, p. 34.
3. Mundy, *Michelle*, p. 78.
4. Andersen, *Barack and Michelle*, p. 96.
5. Ibid.
6. Ibid., p. 95.
7. Brophy, *Michelle Obama*, p. 36.
8. Ibid.
9. Mundy, *Michelle*, p. 84.
10. Andersen, *Barack and Michelle*, p. 97.
11. Mundy, *Michelle*, p. 85.
12. Andersen, *Barack and Michelle*, pp. 97–98.
13. Mundy, *Michelle*, p. 92.
14. Andersen, *Barack and Michelle*, p. 98.
15. Ibid., p. 118.
16. Mundy, *Michelle*, p. 94.
17. Ibid.
18. Andersen, *Barack and Michelle*, p. 121.
19. Colbert, *Michelle Obama*, p. 94.
20. Andersen, *Barack and Michelle*, p. 121.
21. Ibid.
22. Mundy, *Michelle*, p. 95.

23. Ibid., p. 96.
24. Andersen, *Barack and Michelle*, p. 122.
25. Ibid., p. 123.
26. Ibid., p. 124.
27. Ibid.
28. Barack Obama, *The Audacity of Hope: Thoughts on Reclaiming the American Dream*. New York: Crown Publishers, 2006, p. 389.
29. Andersen, *Barack and Michelle*, p. 125.
30. Brophy, *Michelle Obama*, p. 50.
31. Andersen, *Barack and Michelle*, p. 126.

CHAPTER 7

1. Andersen, *Barack and Michelle*, p. 139.
2. Ibid.
3. Ibid., pp. 139–140.
4. Colbert, *Michelle Obama*, p. 110.
5. Andersen, *Barack and Michelle*, p. 140.
6. Obama, *The Audacity of Hope*, p. 391.
7. Andersen, *Barack and Michelle*, p. 141.
8. Mundy, *Michelle*, p. 101.
9. Colbert, *Michelle Obama*, p. 109.
10. Mundy, *Michelle*, p. 111.
11. Andersen, *Barack and Michelle*, p. 150.
12. Ibid., p. 152.

CHAPTER 8

1. Mundy, *Michelle*, p. 122.
2. Andersen, *Barack and Michelle*, p. 161.
3. Mundy, *Michelle*, p. 117.
4. Ibid., p. 115.
5. Colbert, *Michelle Obama*, p. 116.
6. Mundy, *Michelle*, p. 142.
7. Andersen, *Barack and Michelle*, p. 170.

8. Ibid., p. 177.
9. Colbert, *Michelle Obama*, p. 119.
10. Andersen, *Barack and Michelle*, p. 187.
11. Ibid., p. 8.
12. Ibid., p. 187.
13. Ibid., p. 188.
14. Obama, *The Audacity of Hope*, p. 400.
15. Andersen, *Barack and Michelle*, p. 191.
16. Obama, *The Audacity of Hope*, p. 401.
17. Andersen, *Barack and Michelle*, p. 10.
18. Colbert, *Michelle Obama*, p. 121.
19. Mundy, *Michelle*, p. 138.
20. Ibid., pp. 138–139.
21. Andersen, *Barack and Michelle*, p. 199.
22. Ibid., p. 200.
23. Colbert, *Michelle Obama*, p. 123.
24. Andersen, *Barack and Michelle*, p. 198.
25. Colbert, *Michelle Obama*, p. 124.
26. Ibid.
27. Andersen, *Barack and Michelle*, p. 205.
28. Ibid., p. 216.
29. Ibid., p. 217.
30. Ibid., p. 126.
31. Andersen, *Barack and Michelle*, p. 218.
32. Colbert, *Michelle Obama*, p. 126.
33. Andersen, *Barack and Michelle*, p. 227.

CHAPTER 9

1. Andersen, *Barack and Michelle*, p. 229.
2. Mundy, *Michelle*, p. 164.
3. Colbert, *Michelle Obama*, p. 129.
4. Mundy, *Michelle*, p. 170.
5. Ibid.
6. Brophy, *Michelle Obama*, p. 73.

7.   Colbert, *Michelle Obama*, p. 132.
8.   Ibid.
9.   Mundy, *Michelle*, p. 186.
10. Colbert, *Michelle Obama*, p. 135.
11. Andersen, *Barack and Michelle*, p. 264.
12. Mundy, *Michelle*, p. 190.
13. Andersen, *Barack and Michelle*, p. 265.
14. Colbert, *Michelle Obama*, p. 137.
15. Brophy, *Michelle Obama*, p. 89.

CHAPTER 10

1.   Susan Baer, "Michelle's First 100 Days," *Washingtonian*. January 2009: p. 73.

2.   Harriette Cole, "The Real Michelle Obama," *Ebony*. September 2008: p. 84.

3.   Jon Meacham, "Michelle Obama: 'We Just Need Common Sense,'" *Newsweek*. March 19, 2010. http://www.newsweek.com/id/235180.

4.   Robin Givhan, "Michelle Obama Announces More Funding for Military Families in FY 2011 Budget," *Washington Post*. January 27, 2010. http://www.washingtonpost.com/wp-dyn/content/article/2010/01/26/AR2010012603274.html.

5.   Richard Wolffe, "Barack's Rock," *Newsweek*. February 16, 2008. http://www.newsweek.com/id/112849/page/5.

6.   "Michelle Obama's Commencement Address," delivered at the University of California, Merced, *New York Times*. May 16, 2009. http://www.nytimes.com/2009/05/16/us/politics/16text-michelle.html?pagewanted=5&_r=1.

BIBLIOGRAPHY

Andersen, Christopher. *Barack and Michelle: Portrait of an American Marriage*. New York: William Morrow, 2009.

Baer, Susan. "Michelle's First 100 Days." *Washingtonian*, January 2009.

Brophy, David Bergen. *Michelle Obama: Meet the First Lady*. New York: HarperCollins, 2009.

Colbert, David. *Michelle Obama: An American Story*. Boston: Houghton Mifflin Harcourt, 2009.

Cole, Harriette. "The Real Michelle Obama." *Ebony*, September 2008.

Collins, Lauren. "The Other Obama." *New Yorker*, March 10, 2008.

Mundy, Liza. *Michelle: A Biography*. New York: Simon & Schuster, 2008.

Murray, Shailagh. "A Family Tree Rooted in American Soil." *Washington Post*, October 2, 2008. Available online. URL: http://www.washingtonpost.com/wp-dyn/content/story/2008/10/01/ST2008100103245.html.

Obama, Barack. *The Audacity of Hope: Thoughts on Reclaiming the American Dream*. New York: Crown Publishers, 2006.

Swarns, Rachel L., and Jodi Kantor. "In First Lady's Roots, a Complex Path From Slavery." *New York Times*, October 7, 2009. Available online. URL: http://www.nytimes.com/2009/10/08/us/politics/08genealogy.html.

FURTHER RESOURCES

BOOKS

Edwards, Roberta, and Ken Call (illustrator). *Michelle Obama: Mom-in-Chief*. New York: Penguin Group, 2009.

Lightfoot, Elizabeth. *Michelle Obama: First Lady of Hope*. Guilford, Conn.: The Lyons Press, 2009.

Swimmer, Susan. *Michelle Obama: First Lady of Fashion and Style*. New York: Black Dog & Leventhal Publishers, Inc., 2009.

Von Zumbusch, Amelie. *Michelle Obama: Our First Lady*. New York: The Rosen Publishing Group, Inc., 2010.

WEB SITES

Michelle Obama Watch
http://michelleobamawatch.com/

Organizing for America
http://www.barackobama.com/

The White House—First Lady Michelle Obama
http://www.whitehouse.gov/administration/first-lady-michelle-obama

PICTURE CREDITS

INDEX

ABOUT THE AUTHOR

PAUL McCAFFREY graduated from the Millbrook School in Millbrook, New York, and received his bachelor of arts degree from Vassar College in Poughkeepsie, New York. He is an editor at the H.W. Wilson Company, a library reference publisher, where he oversees The Reference Shelf series. Among the titles he has edited or coedited are *The United States Election System*, *Hispanic Americans*, and *The United States Supreme Court*. Some of the other publications he has worked on are *Facts About the Presidents, Eighth Edition*, and *The Tenth Book of Junior Authors & Illustrators*. In addition to *Michelle Obama*, he has written *Ruth Bader Ginsburg* for Chelsea House. Raised in Brookfield, Connecticut, he lives in Brooklyn, New York.

```
TIME         : Sat Jun 09 2012 04:18PM
TERMINAL     : 300
TITLE        : Michelle Obama : First Lad
y / Paul McCaffrey.
CALL NUMBER  : YA B OBAMA  duab
BARCODE      : 22701525082
STATUS       : IN TRANSIT
Received. Belongs at Durham Adult Biogra
phy.
```